# *Truly You*

# *Truly You*

## 90 Devotions on Faith, Feelings, and Friends for Teen Girls

## Sarah Humphrey

*Truly You: 90 Devotions on Faith, Feelings, and Friends for Teen Girls*
© 2025 by Sarah Humphrey

All rights reserved.

Requests for permission to quote from this book should be directed to: Permissions Department, Our Daily Bread Publishing, PO Box 3566, Grand Rapids, MI 49501; or contact us by email at permissionsdept@odbm.org.

Scripture quotations, unless otherwise indicated, are taken from the Holy Bible, New International Version®, NIV®. Copyright © 1973, 1978, 1984, 2011 by Biblica, Inc.™ Used by permission of Zondervan. All rights reserved worldwide. www.zondervan.com.
   Scripture quotations marked CEB are taken from the COMMON ENGLISH BIBLE. © Copyright 2011 COMMON ENGLISH BIBLE. All rights reserved. Used by permission. (www.CommonEnglishBible.com).
   Scripture quotations marked CSB are taken from the Christian Standard Bible®, Copyright © 2017 by Holman Bible Publishers. Used by permission. Christian Standard Bible® and CSB® are federally registered trademarks of Holman Bible Publishers.
   Scripture quotations marked KJV are taken from the Authorized Version, or King James Version, of the Bible.
   Scripture quotations marked NLT are taken from the *Holy Bible*, New Living Translation, copyright © 1996, 2004, 2015 by Tyndale House Foundation. Used by permission of Tyndale House Publishers, Carol Stream, Illinois 60188. All rights reserved.

Interior design by Michael J. Williams

ISBN: 978-1-64070-422-0

**Library of Congress Cataloging-in-Publication Data Available**

*Printed in the United States of America*
25 26 27 28 29 30 31 32 / 8 7 6 5 4 3 2 1

Dedicated to my daughters, Ella and Lucy.
May you always be truly you, in every way God fashioned you.

**Dear Reader,**

Real life can be difficult to fit into the tightly constructed boxes that society has shaped for females no matter our hopes, talents, or gifts. What we see in magazines and on social media gives us glimpses into what we seemingly *should* aspire to be. Sadly, the airbrushed images don't leave much room to process actual feelings, discover guidance toward true answers, and find ourselves without getting into trouble.

Every young woman wants to be known, to be understood, and to belong. That's God's nature in all of us, from baby to granny. We are feelers and creators, and yet we need truth and security to bloom. Where we look for answers can have profound effects on how our hearts beat, what our future looks like, and if our goals become reality. While every girl may not have the same dreams, every girl desires to be loved. It's in our DNA because we are God's beloved.

Topics like identity, fear, grief, and friendship can be tough to talk about. It's not necessarily easy to become a woman! Together we'll wrestle with these themes with honest questions and prayer. When we talk to God, our perspective can be transformed. As followers of Jesus, his Spirit lives in us and his Word directs us.

Through this ninety-day journey, I hope your understanding of God's presence is made real in new ways. After every reading, you'll notice a verse and a prompt to speak, doodle, and write along with a dot journal page. This is your invitation to interact with God's Word.

Speaking and praying the Bible out loud is a great way to memorize truth. If you do, I know you will find good opportunities to search out God's plans for you.

Or perhaps you're an artist and would prefer to draw or doodle about what a verse means to you. Or maybe you simply talk to God in your journal.

I hope you find peace in God, fresh love for the Scriptures, and discover new things about yourself as you work through this book. I am glad I get to walk with you as you add wisdom and joy to your already blooming, beautiful life.

Enjoy the journey,
Sarah

# Contents

| | | |
|---|---|---|
| Day 1: | Live Simply *Psalm 19:7* | 12 |
| Day 2: | Clean Space *Psalm 51:10* | 14 |
| Day 3: | Coffee Date with God *Psalm 46:10* | 16 |
| Day 4: | God's Creation *Habakkuk 3:4* | 18 |
| Day 5: | Precious to God *1 Peter 3:4* | 20 |
| Day 6: | Moving with Him *Acts 17:28* | 22 |
| Day 7: | There Is Hope *Psalm 139:13–14* | 24 |
| Day 8: | Journaling Well *Psalm 55:22* | 26 |
| Day 9: | Doodle Your Day *Romans 12:12* | 28 |
| Day 10: | New Creation *2 Corinthians 5:17* | 30 |
| Day 11: | You Are Loved *Zephaniah 3:17* | 32 |
| Day 12: | Don't Quit *Hebrews 12:1* | 34 |
| Day 13: | Identity for You *Philippians 1:6* | 36 |
| Day 14: | Friendship for Good *Proverbs 27:9* | 38 |
| Day 15: | Social Media Woes *Deuteronomy 30:19–20* | 40 |
| Day 16: | Forgiving Others *Matthew 6:14* | 42 |
| Day 17: | Jealous Eyes *Proverbs 14:30* | 44 |
| Day 18: | Boundaries for Good *Galatians 5:13* | 46 |
| Day 19: | Slow Down *Proverbs 4:26* | 48 |
| Day 20: | Decisions, Decisions *Proverbs 3:5–6* | 50 |
| Day 21: | Comparison Battles *James 4:8* | 52 |
| Day 22: | Competition Fails *2 Timothy 2:5* | 54 |
| Day 23: | Seen and Heard *Psalm 17:6* | 56 |
| Day 24: | Friendship Changes *Proverbs 17:17* | 58 |
| Day 25: | Candid Conversations *Proverbs 27:17* | 60 |
| Day 26: | Letting Go in Friendship *Proverbs 12:26* | 62 |

| | | |
|---|---|---|
| Day 27: | What Do You Mean? *Colossians 4:6* | 64 |
| Day 28: | Wait a Minute *Psalm 31:15* | 66 |
| Day 29: | Working for the Lord *Colossians 3:23* | 68 |
| Day 30: | Live Fully *John 15:16* | 70 |
| Day 31: | Expectation Troubles *Isaiah 55:8–9* | 72 |
| Day 32: | Think on These Things *Philippians 4:8* | 74 |
| Day 33: | Quality over Quantity *Philippians 1:9–10* | 76 |
| Day 34: | He's Cute *Psalm 37:4* | 78 |
| Day 35: | Needs of the Heart *Matthew 6:33* | 80 |
| Day 36: | Speak Up *Job 33:3* | 82 |
| Day 37: | It's a Date *Ephesians 6:2–3* | 84 |
| Day 38: | It's Official *Psalm 16:6* | 86 |
| Day 39: | Breathe and Pray *1 Peter 5:7* | 88 |
| Day 40: | Healthy Choices Win *1 Corinthians 10:31* | 90 |
| Day 41: | Be Kind to Yourself *Romans 2:4* | 92 |
| Day 42: | Honesty Brings Connection *Matthew 18:20* | 94 |
| Day 43: | Will You Still Love Me? *Lamentations 3:22–23* | 96 |
| Day 44: | Which Path? *Psalm 119:105* | 98 |
| Day 45: | Hormone Messages *Genesis 1:27* | 100 |
| Day 46: | Do Not Be Afraid *Joshua 1:9* | 102 |
| Day 47: | Fear of Missing Out *Hebrews 13:8* | 104 |
| Day 48: | Ask for Help *Hebrews 10:24–25* | 106 |
| Day 49: | Burnt Out? *Matthew 11:28–30* | 108 |
| Day 50: | Nothing Is Impossible *Luke 1:30* | 110 |
| Day 51: | Respect Elders *1 Peter 5:5* | 112 |
| Day 52: | Mentoring Guides *1 Corinthians 11:1* | 114 |
| Day 53: | Speaking Well *Luke 6:45* | 116 |
| Day 54: | Goals and Dreams *Ephesians 3:20–21* | 118 |
| Day 55: | Sibling Love *Romans 7:4* | 120 |
| Day 56: | Sleeping Sorrows *Psalm 121:3–4* | 122 |
| Day 57: | No One Better *Isaiah 40:25* | 124 |
| Day 58: | Be a Peacemaker *Matthew 5:9* | 126 |
| Day 59: | Comfort Matters *2 Corinthians 1:3* | 128 |

| | | |
|---|---|---|
| Day 60: | Chosen with Style *Colossians 3:12* | 130 |
| Day 61: | Diligence Is Good *2 Peter 3:14* | 132 |
| Day 62: | God Is Faithful *2 Timothy 1:7* | 134 |
| Day 63: | Grief Heals *John 16:33* | 136 |
| Day 64: | Help My Unbelief *Mark 9:24* | 138 |
| Day 65: | Joy of the Lord *Nehemiah 8:10* | 140 |
| Day 66: | Serve the Little Ones *Luke 18:16* | 142 |
| Day 67: | Kindness Wins *Proverbs 16:24* | 144 |
| Day 68: | Be Real *Song of Songs 4:7* | 146 |
| Day 69: | Be an Example *Proverbs 4:18* | 148 |
| Day 70: | Do What's Right *1 Peter 3:14* | 150 |
| Day 71: | A Season for Everything *Ecclesiastes 3:1* | 152 |
| Day 72: | Content in Jesus *1 Timothy 6:6* | 154 |
| Day 73: | Silly Sometimes *Luke 6:21* | 156 |
| Day 74: | Love Boundaries *Proverbs 16:32* | 158 |
| Day 75: | The Shame Game *Psalm 22:4–5* | 160 |
| Day 76: | Learning Differently *Genesis 1:27* | 162 |
| Day 77: | Detox *Psalm 51:7* | 164 |
| Day 78: | Worthiness in Christ *Hebrews 10:35–36* | 166 |
| Day 79: | Sadness Seasons *Psalm 30:11* | 168 |
| Day 80: | Integrity Satisfies *1 Timothy 4:12* | 170 |
| Day 81: | Garden Growing *Genesis 2:8* | 172 |
| Day 82: | I AM *Exodus 3:14* | 174 |
| Day 83: | Hope Heals *Proverbs 13:12* | 176 |
| Day 84: | Bite Your Tongue *Proverbs 18:21* | 178 |
| Day 85: | Think of Others *Philippians 2:3–5* | 180 |
| Day 86: | Be Kind to Your Parents *Ephesians 4:32* | 182 |
| Day 87: | Honor Your Body *1 Corinthians 6:19–20* | 184 |
| Day 88: | Love Carefully *1 Corinthians 13:1* | 186 |
| Day 89: | Be You *Ephesians 1:4–6* | 188 |
| Day 90: | Be Well *Colossians 2:6–7* | 190 |

# DAY 1

# Live Simply

The world will tell you to buy more, be more, do more . . .

I am here to tell you the opposite. Staying up on trends is often unsatisfying. Busy is not necessarily better. It's sometimes exhausting. Hustle isn't the formula for success. More is often not even fulfilling! We do need to live, and move, and explore, yes. It's easy to get sluggish if we don't keep moving, but we can also get overwhelmed if we carry too much.

My best solution to this high-tech and fast-paced life is learning how to be present, live simply, and then give practically. This has brought me joy, peace, and progress.

The first step to living well is to be still in God's presence and then let him show you how loved you are. Take ten minutes to look up and read Scripture passages about who God made you to be and how much he cares.

You can know who you are because you are God's child, and the Bible gives you a clear idea at what a life in God is like. With God's vision of you in mind, you're equipped to choose what you really love, and let the rest fall away. You can squish depression and anxiety by knowing you don't have to have everything and be everything in order to be loved. That means you can minimize your materials and schedule so that you can maximize your life, your real friendships, and your gifts.*

When you start small and authentic, God will nourish you in the process. You won't regret it!

---

\* Sometimes when anxiety and depression hang on longer than we'd like, we need more than a few strategies to help. If this is you, please talk to a parent, school counselor, or other trusted adult to find additional help.

**Speak it. Doodle it. Write it out.**

The law of the Lord is perfect, refreshing the soul. The statutes of the Lord are trustworthy, making wise the simple.
—Psalm 19:7

**Say a prayer.**

*Jesus, I want to live a life that honors you and who you've created me to be. Help me put away distractions and engage fully in all that you have for me. I love you. Amen.*

# DAY 2

# Clean Space

When I cuddle up with a good devotional, I love a clean space! I'm not sure about you, but when my surroundings are full of yesterday's unfinished chores, I get a little irritable.

Did you know science proves that clutter actually creates anxiety? Decluttering and freshening up help make order in our living spaces and in our hearts. And that clear environment gives us balance and clarity to dig deep with God while also getting cozy in our surroundings. It's nice to know that we have open space to breathe if we run into big feelings we need to work through.

If you've ever watched a flower bloom, a butterfly metamorphose, or a ballerina dance, you'll notice she transforms from the inside out. While the petals are wrapped around the seeds, or the cocoon is dark, or the dancer is breathing, I like to think she is preparing for her new adventure. So, as I get ready to spend significant time with God—I clean. It helps me get ready to hear him clearly!

Take ten minutes today to declutter your space. What are a few things you can get rid of that you don't need? Any trash lying around? Do your clothes need to be put away? What can you do at this moment to make room in your space so that you are ready to dive into God's Word? Taking a few minutes to let go of some physical things can also help you release some of the emotional clutter. All of which makes more room in your heart for God.

### Speak it. Doodle it. Write it out.

Create a clean heart for me, God; put a new, faithful spirit deep inside me!
—Psalm 51:10 CEB

### Say a prayer.

*God, you love to spend time with me, and I want to learn how to spend time with you! Help me clear the clutter in my life, so I can be ready to dive deep with you. I want to hear your thoughts and learn from your Word. Amen.*

# DAY 3

# Coffee Date with God

Where do you feel most safe and happy? Maybe a comfy coffee shop? Perhaps the warm vibe and the smell of java feels like home. Or maybe you prefer a certain spot in the woods. Or a nook in your grandma's house.

Take time today to find a quiet, safe place to cozy up with a hot drink and a blanket. Then ask God to purposefully show himself to you. Often it's in these simple, small moments that we can hear God speak to us most clearly.

When we intentionally quiet ourselves and set our heart to listening, we give him room to speak so we can engage in his desires for us. It's really that simple. Pause and listen. He has good plans for you! Then, share your feelings with him. He cares about your details. Allow him to give you peace and joy in the conversation. Open your Bible and read through a psalm or two. If you get distracted, that's okay. Write down the distraction and go back to focusing on God. Enjoy learning the art of quieting your thoughts and listening for his thoughts. It might feel a little awkward at first, but as you go through this devotional, you'll start to see the beauty of waiting on Jesus. There's no better place to refresh than to have a coffee date with God.

### Speak it. Doodle it. Write it out.

Be still, and know that I am God!
—Psalm 46:10 NLT

### Say a prayer.

*Jesus, I want to learn how to listen in stillness. Will you show me how to read your Word and speak my thoughts honestly? Even though you know my needs before I say them, I want to practice sharing with you on purpose. Amen.*

# DAY 4

# God's Creation

Sometimes we need some sunshine, a flower, or another part of God's creation to refresh us. Fluorescent lights above us and screens in our faces can make us feel anxious and uneasy. Go outside today and spend some time in nature to break up the glaring flow of electronics! If it's nice outdoors, take a walk with a friend. If it's cold, sit on the porch for a few minutes and embrace the chill. Feel the coolness in your bones, and exhale warm air into the wind. If it's hot, take a dip at the local pool or park. Relish in the sun shining peacefully on your face while filling you with nourishment and nutrients. Who doesn't love some vitamin D?

In a world of computers and phones, we need God's creation. It's good to take the time to enjoy a few minutes to breathe fresh air, to nourish our souls with nature, and to live in the beauty that God designed. Find something in nature that matches your favorite color. Go look in the clouds for hidden shapes and beauty. Smell a flower or a plant nearby.

What are some of your favorite ways to enjoy the outdoors? How does God speak to you through nature? What is your favorite season of the year and why?

### Speak it. Doodle it. Write it out.

His coming is as brilliant as the sunrise.
—Habakkuk 3:4 NLT

### Say a prayer.

*God, thank you for creating this beautiful world! It helps to know how small I am and how big you are. Thank you for fresh air to breathe, for the beauty of trees, for the sun in the sky, and even for the rain. Amen.*

DAY 5

# Precious to God

Ever had a day when you looked in the mirror and just felt "blah"? We often measure our mood by what we think we see in our reflection. And you know what? Society isn't helpful in this area. We feel the pressure of measuring our worth against the face we see in the mirror, the number we see on a scale, or the way our clothes fit.

Unfortunately, this is a result of the curse of Eve. Her basic problem was believing the lie that what God had given her was not enough. Like Eve, we search to feel loved and accepted, to have or be more, and we often go straight to our appearance.

We look at our face and shame ourselves, wanting better eyelashes or a different nose. Maybe clearer skin or thicker hair. But no matter what you think is beautiful on the outside, it never compares with the beauty of a quiet spirit. Don't believe me? Check out one of my favorite Scriptures, and one that I dig deep to relish in every day. First Peter 3:4 says, "You should clothe yourselves instead with the beauty that comes from within, the unfading beauty of a gentle and quiet spirit, which is so precious to God" (NLT).

Precious to God. That's who you are.

So, the next time you look in the mirror, look to God and say, "Thank you for making me beautiful in your sight." Make it a habit until you believe it.

### Speak it. Doodle it. Write it out.

You should clothe yourselves instead with the beauty that comes from within, the unfading beauty of a gentle and quiet spirit, which is so precious to God.
—1 Peter 3:4 NLT

### Say a prayer.

*God, thank you for creating me. Thank you for this body that you have made. Though I can look around and compare myself to others, I pray that you would do a deep work in my heart so I can fully love myself just as you've made me. Amen.*

# DAY 6

# Moving with Him

Part of loving ourselves definitely means moving our bodies! There have been many days when I've woken up a little bit grumpy, or irritable, or simply not my best. Sometimes we get that stuck feeling that doesn't easily go away. It's kind of like being moody but also like feeling frustrated, and everyone around us seems to be not what we need at the moment.

You know what can often help that? A walk or a jog, a little time with a jump rope or an hour at the ballet barre. Moving our God-given bodies not only can help us fight emotional unsettledness, but it also can fill us with happiness and purpose. When I get out of my slump and put my body in motion, I usually find plenty of good ideas, productivity, and energy.

What's true for our physical bodies is true for our faith too. Scripture tells us that God lives in us, but "faith by itself isn't enough" (James 2:17 NLT). Just like when we don't exercise, if we don't work on our faith in Jesus, we can be stuck in our dead, grumpy, depressed, or anxious ways. But when we set ourselves in motion, making the conscious choice to move with God, we change the whole course of our day. We can set aside our old feelings and tangled thoughts and engage with the discipline and love of the God who makes us come alive.

### Speak it. Doodle it. Write it out.

For in him we live and move and exist. As some of your own poets have said, "We are his offspring."
—Acts 17:28 NLT

### Say a prayer.

*God, thank you for giving me new life in you. Even when I'm not feeling motivated, help me to move with you and to change my mindset by honoring my body. I want to be healthy, whole, and alive in you. Amen.*

# DAY 7

# There Is Hope

Nearly thirty percent of teenage young women seriously consider hurting themselves every year.* It's a statistic that makes me want to climb through the page and hug every single one of you reading these words. You see, if three in ten teenage women are struggling this deeply, it's possible that one of those struggling teenagers is you. If so, I am so glad you're here. I know you can't physically see me, but know that I am praying for you and that you are loved and needed beyond measure.

When the world around you says you are only important, loved, or accepted when you perform, succeed, or look a certain way, it can be really difficult to resist fitting in so you can find where you belong. *But you do belong.* God chose you before time to live and love in this season of history. And even though life might be tough, and you may be hurting, or a friend might be struggling, know that God is always with you. He is our hope. That's what these ninety devotions are all about—finding the God of hope right where you are.

At this point, you're seven days into this devotional, and it's time to celebrate a bit. Write down a few things you've learned so far. Thank God for those nuggets of knowledge, and lean into them. There is hope and life to be lived fully, as you realize that you are needed and valuable to the world around you.

---

\* Emily Baumgaertner, "How Many Teenage Girls Deliberately Harm Themselves? Nearly 1 in 4, Survey Finds," July 2, 2018, https://www.nytimes.com/2018/07/02/health/self-harm-teenagers-cdc.html.

### Speak it. Doodle it. Write it out.

For you created my inmost being; you knit me together in my mother's womb. I praise you because I am fearfully and wonderfully made; your works are wonderful, I know that full well.
—Psalm 139:13–14

### Say a prayer.

*God, thank you for giving me life. I pray that I will hear you clearly, receive your love, and make the most of my God-given life. I am so grateful to belong to you. Amen.*

# DAY 8

# Journaling Well

Have you ever sat down to think about how God created your life unique and full of wonder? Just like he makes millions of varieties of flowers, he also made you and your life beautiful and special. When you plant a seed, there is growth and surprise in store as it gets fully rooted and starts to take shape, size, and color. That's how your purpose in God grows too. When God plants you, it might feel like you're in dark soil for a bit. As he waters and brings sunshine, you start to bloom with him.

Your emotions are a big part of life's process. It's easy for all of us to have a variety of thoughts, feelings, struggles, and joys in just one day. Your body is changing, and your relationships are transitioning too. That's why giving your emotions to God can be such a healthy, helpful, and creative part of your journey. Talking to God through journaling and art can be just the creative release you need when life becomes heavy, overwhelming, or even when it's just normal and average. God loves honesty. He values how you feel and always has a listening ear available.

Take some time today to grab a journal and jot down your feelings. No need to edit it or even use punctuation. Let the feelings flow, and know that everything you put on the page gets all of those grumblings out of your head. Once those grumblings are out, your life will bloom where it has been planted.

### Speak it. Doodle it. Write it out.

Cast your cares on the Lord and he will sustain you;
he will never let the righteous be shaken.
—Psalm 55:22

### Say a prayer.

*Jesus, thank you for loving me and all of my feelings. Help me to express myself honestly, so that I can release what is in my heart. Amen.*

# DAY 9

# Doodle Your Day

Ever had a day when you don't exactly know what's wrong, but something is just wrong? Sometimes we push emotions to the side or shut down our hearts when we get angry or irritated. Maybe you've even been told that anger or sadness is bad, and so it's difficult to know how or when to express yourself.

Or perhaps certain days you might want something to go a specific way, and it doesn't. Like maybe you really wanted some sunshine, and it rained. Or perhaps you could have really used a cozy thunderstorm to cuddle up in a comfy spot, but the sun was blazing hot. If you've ever walked through a garden, you know that flowers need both sun and rain to bloom. And people do too. We need both the good things to give us the strength to stretch up and the bad to help us dig deep.

What are some of the feelings or thoughts you've had this week? Does anything specific stick out to you as good or difficult? Can you think of some adjectives that describe what was going on in your heart and mind as these events were happening? Choose a word or phrase that speaks to you. Write it down, then decorate it and color it in. No one even needs to see it if you don't want them to. So, grab some markers, and let those feelings flow.

### Speak it. Doodle it. Write it out.

Be joyful in hope, patient in affliction, faithful in prayer.
—Romans 12:12

### Say a prayer.

*Holy Spirit, thank you for loving me in the midst of my messiness. I have such big feelings sometimes. Give me wisdom as I sort them out. Amen.*

# DAY 10

# New Creation

Maybe you are still thinking about what this Christianity thing is all about, and you're wondering what life with Jesus looks like. Second Corinthians 5:17 says that when you became a Christian, you became a new person!

The Bible teaches us that no matter what we've done or how we've messed up, when we trust and believe in him, Jesus makes us new. His perfect life washes away our imperfect one, and by believing and learning to love God, we also learn to love our new lives. That sounds like a pretty good gift to me.

There have been plenty of times I have sinned as a Christian. I've said something regretful, I've been impatient, and I've even intentionally chosen something easy instead of what was right. That surely doesn't make me feel new. Thankfully, the Holy Spirit convicts me in these times and reminds me how to change. He encourages me to pray, ask for and receive forgiveness, and then try again. From this perspective, we can see Christ's newness in us.

It takes time, and being a Christian isn't always easy. It's worth it, though, and so are you. By challenging yourself to spend time getting to know Jesus, you will find more beauty, freedom, and joy than you ever knew before. So, take the time to do that. Stop and pray for five minutes, and ask Jesus to come into a few of your struggling spaces and bring new life. God loves it when you spend devoted time with him.

**Speak it. Doodle it. Write it out.**

This means that anyone who belongs to Christ has become a new person. The old life is gone; a new life has begun!
—2 Corinthians 5:17 NLT

**Say a prayer.**

*God, thank you for creating me and loving me. Help me to spend time purposely with you so that I can learn how you make all things new. Amen.*

## DAY 11

# You Are Loved

In a world that tells you to constantly do, win, or conquer, it might be surprising that success looks different for different people, and often will surprise you in unexpected ways. There was once a time I felt God telling me that I would only succeed if I took a nap. He said resting in him was the goal (Psalm 37:7). How ironic is that?

Even when outward success is well-deserved, God is the one who brings us through, who labors on our behalf, and who helps us. Whenever you get side-tracked by thinking that your performance determines your value, remember that you are not what you do. This can be tricky because winning is fun and feels good. No one likes to lose, and yet losing teaches us different values like humility, sportsmanship, and patience.

No exam, spot on the team, or popularity contest tells us who we are. We are who God made us to be, we are loved by the Creator of the universe, and he determines our value. This is important to remember while we are navigating the more difficult times in our lives.

Everyone God has made is loved by him. So, the next time you win or you lose, remember this: No matter what, you are loved. You are valuable. You are special.

### Speak it. Doodle it. Write it out.

The Lord your God is among you, a warrior who saves. He will rejoice over you with gladness. He will be quiet in his love. He will delight in you with singing.
—Zephaniah 3:17 csb

### Say a prayer.

*Father, thank you for giving me rest. Remind me of your faithfulness and kindness. Help me to receive your heart and thoughts toward me. Amen.*

# DAY 12

# Don't Quit

I despised running when I was young. Cardio was so hard and miserable. Some people on my track team ran with ease and could go miles after a full day of school. I was always trying to catch my breath and not feel like I was dying. I quit the team just weeks after starting.

Sometimes life is a mind game, and that means doing something you don't like because you know it's good for you. Running is one of those things for me. Eventually, I learned new ways to deal with pain and put my sneakers back on.

I'm not a fast runner, and I don't run marathons. I have made plenty of strides, though, and I am learning to embrace the pain in ways that made me give up before and to breathe properly while running. I don't quit now and am slowly increasing my speed and distance. My mind is set on the prize of finishing, no matter how well I do. What does running your race look like for you? Do you have something you've quit previously that you'd like to, or feel like you should, try again?

Consider Paul's call to endurance in the Hebrews passage at the end of this devotion. Paul encourages us not to give up, even when it's hard and even when we don't win. Start small but try again, with the goal not to quit, and see what God shows you.

### Speak it. Doodle it. Write it out.

*Let us lay aside every hindrance and the sin that so easily ensnares us. Let us run with endurance the race that lies before us.*
—Hebrews 12:1 CSB

### Say a prayer.

*Jesus, you give me strength! As I work hard and put in the time, I ask that you would bless my efforts. Amen.*

# DAY 13

# Identity for You

The world and the people in it have opinions, suggestions, and advice for you. They might even fill your mind and heart with desires, hopes, dreams, and fears that can be counterfeits of God's true calling for you. That's why the Word of God is so important. Knowing what God says is true, and knowing who Jesus is and what he did, will be the everlasting security for your soul. No matter what happens around you, God is with you. He loves you. He has a plan for you and will complete it. And he can transform your heart and life when you come to him in humility and prayer.

None of us will ever be perfect. We're all trying to do the best we can with what we have and know. But we can count on Scripture to point us in the right direction, and we can hear God when we come to him with a genuine and honest heart. When we're patient with our lives and circumstances and persistent in listening to his voice, we can be sure that his perfect will happens in our lives . . . even if it isn't what we expect.

God is good. He knows us deeply and loves us well. We can trust his plans for us, even when outside opinions and accusations tell us otherwise.

### Speak it. Doodle it. Write it out.

I am sure of this, that he who started a good work in you will carry it on to completion until the day of Christ Jesus.
—Philippians 1:6 CSB

### Say a prayer.

*God, you have the best plans for me. Help me hear your voice and know your heart so I can walk in your goodness. Amen.*

## DAY 14

# Friendship for Good

Everyone feels lonely at times. There is a lot of pressure to fit in and be liked. To perform in order to be noticed. Finding a friend who really cares and is loyal is such a gift. Maybe you don't have a friend like that yet or maybe you do. If you don't, you can always be that kind of friend to someone else. There's a saying "If you want a friend, be a friend," and I would say that's true.

Investing in friendship in a godly way can look like encouraging one another, asking your friends how they're doing (more than just on the surface), and praying for one another. It's always nice to know that a friend is in your corner.

What can you do to go a little bit deeper with your friendships this week? How can you support your peers? You might be surprised at how encouraged you'll feel when you take friendship to the next level by offering genuine care and a thoughtful question or two. Be the friend that you want to have—give a kind word to and say a prayer for someone you love. A hug would be a really great idea too!

### Speak it. Doodle it. Write it out.

Oil and incense bring joy to the heart, and the sweetness of a friend is better than self-counsel.
—Proverbs 27:9 CSB

### Say a prayer.

*Jesus, help me be a good friend. I want to love like you love and care for others the way you care for me. Amen.*

# DAY 15

# Social Media Woes

Selfie after selfie. Snapshot after snapshot. BeReal. TikTok. Snapchat. It's one photo after another of FOMO. Life on a screen can be the quickest way to celebrate and also the quickest route to depression, ungratefulness, and anxiety. What we see on a screen is only one piece of reality.

There is something to be said for closing down your apps for a day or two. Some families take Sundays away from screens. Sometimes we need to take a little more time than that. Technology is not necessarily a bad thing, but more often than not, social media creates underlying issues more than it creates peace. What we can feel when we see someone else's photo is what we missed out on, or where we weren't included. Sometimes it can also invite comparisons of what we don't have or what we don't get to do.

Even though all of life seems to value the screen, it's a really good idea to leave that screen behind at times. Try it today. Turn off your phone for two hours and talk to a friend in person. Don't turn on your phone while hanging out with them. Look at them face-to-face and truly connect. If a friend isn't close by, surprise her by sending a handwritten note in the mail. There are a lot of options for how to spend your time. Just remember that doomscrolling can be one of the fastest ways to waste your precious time. Choose wisely!

## Speak it. Doodle it. Write it out.

This day I call the heavens and the earth as witnesses against you that I have set before you life and death, blessings and curses. Now choose life, so that you and your children may live and that you may love the Lord your God, listen to his voice, and hold fast to him. For the Lord is your life.
—Deuteronomy 30:19–20

## Say a prayer.

*Jesus, please remind me of my value in you. Help me stay focused, have proper boundaries with technology, and refresh my soul in your presence. Amen.*

## DAY 16

# Forgiving Others

Sometimes people do things that hurt us. Friends. A parent or coach. A sibling or even a boyfriend. No one is perfect, and the reality is that we are unlikely to get through life without someone hurting our feelings or wronging us.

Certain times people purposefully go out of their way to betray us or embarrass us. That usually hurts the absolute worst. In other situations, it's an accident. We've all had bad days and unintentionally taken it out on someone we love. We live in a world filled with people who are going through some sort of hardship or difficulty. You can take the brunt of every single one of their faulty actions, but that doesn't mean the pain has to ruin you or make you bitter.

The important thing to remember when working through forgiveness is that God is with us through every hurt and every problem. We can receive his grace and give grace away. If we ask, he will help us process what happened and decide how to react in a way that's best for everyone involved. Who do you need to forgive? Or who might you need to apologize to and ask for forgiveness? Learning to forgive is a lifelong process, but practicing now can set you up for an emotionally healthy life.

### Speak it. Doodle it. Write it out.

For if you forgive other people when they sin against you, your heavenly Father will also forgive you.
—Matthew 6:14

### Say a prayer.

*Father God, when I am hurt, remind me of your truth, grace, and mercy toward me. Show me how to forgive others as you have forgiven me. Amen.*

# DAY 17

# Jealous Eyes

Pretend you're walking down the hall, minding your business, heading to class. You're not feeling all that great about your hair. Then, all of a sudden, your friend shows up with the latest haircut and unintentionally ruins your day. Your hair feels even more funky, disheveled, and flat. You want to hide, you want to be mad, you just feel blah.

The good news is you have options in how you react. The temptation will be to burn with anger, feel embarrassed, or possibly get even. For what, you ask? If you're like me, I'm not really sure all the time.

No matter what the reason, take a breath. It's just a bad hair day for you and a great one for her. It happens to us all. Whether it's a haircut, a great outfit, a new ride, or even a good grade, someone will always have something we want and don't have. The important thing to remember is that we get to choose what we focus on.

Life is going to throw you opportunities to see the goodness in others and celebrate, even when you don't feel your best. In all reality, it takes a mature person to celebrate for others when life feels a bit off or incomplete. But taking the opportunity to do that will change your pain into progress. Tomorrow is a new hair day, so don't let today's bad one create hate in your heart.

## Speak it. Doodle it. Write it out.

A peaceful mind gives life to the body, but jealousy rots the bones.
—Proverbs 14:30 CEB

### Say a prayer.

*God, I want to live fully in your love. Whether jealousy, envy, or fear wants to grip my heart, please remind me that I can choose to celebrate for others, and that you celebrate me and care for me on good days and bad. Amen.*

# DAY 18

# Boundaries for Good

Forgiveness and boundaries can sometimes feel like an oxymoron—a kind of ironic contradiction. But the reality is, just because you forgive someone doesn't mean you let that person back into your life with the same amount of trust.

We can look at all kinds of things that deserve forgiveness. Maybe the incident was an accident, a mistake, or a onetime offense that was out of the ordinary. *Yet maybe it was not.* It could be that this person keeps doing the same thing over and over with the same amount of disrespect. That's when Jesus asks us to speak up, tell the truth, and be a voice to make sure the offense doesn't happen again.

A lot of small, trivial incidents can and should be shaken off. But sometimes a boundary is in order, and you should feel the strength and the courage to be able to say so. Forgiving doesn't mean continually allowing other people's offenses. It means speaking the truth in a way that everyone can experience conviction and better choices. And if the other person continues in their harmful behavior, we have the option to walk away from the relationship.

Have you had to forgive and/or set a boundary with anyone lately? How did it go? If it went well, thank God! If it didn't, perhaps seek the advice of an adult who can debrief with you. Sometimes boundaries are really tough to navigate, but God (and adults) can help.

### Speak it. Doodle it. Write it out.

You were called to freedom, brothers and sisters; only don't let this freedom be an opportunity to indulge your selfish impulses, but serve each other through love.
—Galatians 5:13 CEB

### Say a prayer.

*Jesus, help me to be brave with my boundaries. Give me wisdom and understanding, conviction and courage. Help me to speak up and forgive well. Amen.*

# DAY 19

# Slow Down

One of the best pieces of advice I've ever received is, "Slow down and think it through." Ever notice how when you try to rush through things, whether you're making a decision or running after a desire of your heart, your speed can actually make things more complicated?

Moving too fast can cause hiccups, trips, or accidents that could have been avoided. It's like running over rough, unfamiliar ground. If we race after what we want in order to relieve some sort of pain or fill a perceived need, we might twist a metaphorical ankle and land in the pits. Or we might end up lost and on the wrong trail. Thank goodness that God wants to help us and will generously give us wisdom when we ask.

If you've ever heard of Solomon, you know that he was a king who specifically prayed for God's wisdom to help lead people well. And God gave it to him. Wisdom helped Solomon make some really good decisions and also made him very wealthy. Unfortunately, he didn't follow through with God's wisdom all the way to the end, and that caused his downfall. You do not want to repeat Solomon's mistakes.

If you need a reminder to slow down, consider writing Proverbs 4:26 on your bathroom mirror, or put it on your lock screen. When you see it, take a deep breath. The next time you're in a rush, look at it and consider this lesson: there is no need to hurry.

### Speak it. Doodle it. Write it out.

Watch your feet on the way, and all your paths will be secure.
—Proverbs 4:26 CEB

### Say a prayer.

*Heavenly Father, I ask for your wisdom. Help me to slow down and think things through. I want to be guided by your Word and your Spirit. Amen.*

# DAY 20

# Decisions, Decisions

Ever had a tough decision to think through? The decision can feel like a whirlwind in your mind, taking you around and around a topic until you are plain sick of thinking about it. Your heart even races as you worry.

When you want to fret, consider praying instead. When anxiety or decisions fatigue me and plague me, I know I can always talk to God. Feeling heard is one of the quickest ways to calm down. What are you concerned about right now? God wants to hear about it. Even if you think your dilemma is too small or too big, he loves listening to your thoughts and worries, your fears and your decisions. He wants to hear what's on your heart.

Knowing which way to go can sometimes feel very complicated. But God is the best sounding board there is. Getting all your thoughts, concerns, feelings, ideas, and fears out of your mouth and into his hands is the best way to show God you trust him. We don't always understand everything God asks us to do, but we know that he will guide us when we ask him to.

So, let's start now. Take a few minutes and pray. Talk to God about something big or maybe small, and know that he listens and cares.

### Speak it. Doodle it. Write it out.

Trust in the LORD with all your heart and lean not on your own understanding; in all your ways submit to him, and he will make your paths straight.
—Proverbs 3:5–6

### Say a prayer.

*Jesus, there are always choices to make, and I trust you. Please help me navigate opportunities with your peace, knowing that I can always come to you for help. Amen.*

DAY 21

# Comparison Battles

We tend to want what we don't have. If your hair is curly, perhaps you want it to be straight. If you're short, maybe you wish you were tall. If you aren't in great physical shape, maybe you have dreams to become athletic. Some things in life we can change, and others we can't. You might never get curly hair or grow taller, but you could become more athletic. You could start lifting weights or hop into an exercise class.

Comparison can be a difficult game when we want something that is unattainable or unnatural for us to have. Perhaps you want those curls, so you get a perm. It very well might not turn out like the natural curls of your friend.

We can find deeper joy by letting go of comparison and embracing who we actually are. Sometimes you have to find what makes you thrive. Comparison can be an arrow pointing to where you need to connect with yourself and give yourself some grace, and where you can go deeper with God. If you're tempted to compare, make a bracelet or wear a piece of jewelry that reminds you of God's love for you. Jesus doesn't promise that we'll get everything we hope for like those natural bouncy curls, but he does promise to be with us as we find and embrace the beautiful things he made in each one of us.

### Speak it. Doodle it. Write it out.

Come near to God and he will come near to you.
—James 4:8

### Say a prayer.

*God, please bring me peace. Help me to discover and celebrate all the ways you have made me, and may I live fully according to your design for me. Amen.*

# DAY 22

# Competition Fails

Sometimes everything can feel like a competition. How many likes did your social media post receive? How many votes did you get for homecoming? Who picked or didn't pick you for their team? Life can feel like a rat race, and competition is one of the things the Bible warns us about. "Do nothing out of selfish ambition or vain conceit. Rather, in humility value others above yourselves, not looking to your own interests but each of you to the interests of the others" (Philippians 2:3–4).

Competition may not feel selfish at the time, but when you try to one-up someone, you might hurt a friend, do something rude you wish you hadn't, or even injure yourself. If you are competing because you're angry, jealous, or want to prove yourself the winner, you will likely end up disappointed. This doesn't mean you can't have fun and be the best you can be, but it should encourage you to be careful of those around you. When it comes to competition, consider this a healthy warning. Think about others' needs as more important than your own, and have fun doing something together. It will bring about the happiness and improvement you desire.

**Speak it. Doodle it. Write it out.**

Similarly, anyone who competes as an athlete does not receive the victor's crown except by competing according to the rules.
—2 Timothy 2:5

**Say a prayer.**

*Jesus, help me to be a person who enjoys healthy competition—spurring on myself and others to do good things. Teach me how to be a teammate and to value the needs of others. Amen.*

# DAY 23

# Seen and Heard

Selfies, social media, calls, and texts. Life is flooded with people wanting to be seen and heard. Maybe that's you. Maybe you don't think you are known well enough by your family members or friends, so you reach for other ways to be validated. This isn't necessarily a bad thing. It's good to receive encouraging words from friends and family. It's important to know that you are loved and valued. However, if you find yourself going to unprecedented lengths to be acknowledged or doing things just to be noticed, you might scale back and think about your why. What motivates you to do what you do?

Instead of consulting online gurus and the number of likes on our posts, we can turn to God for his approval and advice. Even though God is invisible, talking to him is the best way to be validated. When we reach out to God in prayer, he listens to us and answers. Yes, praying might feel weird—like you don't know what to say, or how to say it right. But God loves you and doesn't care how, when, or why you come to him. So today, perhaps before going to a screen or to a friend, sit down for a few minutes of alone time with the One who loves to hear you speak.

### Speak it. Doodle it. Write it out.

I call on you, my God, for you will answer me; turn your ear to me and hear my prayer.
—Psalm 17:6

### Say a prayer.

*God, thank you for seeing me and knowing me. Please encourage me to pray and speak to you. Remind me of your comfort and care for me. Amen.*

# DAY 24

# Friendship Changes

Ever had a good friend morph into someone you barely recognize? Maybe you were besties, sharing friendship and life, struggles and joys. And then out of the blue, your friend makes a turn, abandoning you at the curb, leaving you feeling a bit unbalanced or even betrayed.

It hurts.

People change. Sometimes change is a good thing, like growth and learning. But sometimes it's hard. When our friendships are challenged or become distant, our self-esteem can crumble. What's important to remember in these situations comes straight from Scripture: "A friend loves at all times" (Proverbs 17:17).

No matter what happens, a good friend finds a way to love, even through adversity and transition. It doesn't mean the relationship stays exactly the same, it just means that your respect, honesty, and care for your friend doesn't change. Over the next few years, you and your friends will go through a lot of transitions, whether that's moving to a new neighborhood, trying a new sport or class, or transforming your physical appearance.

If you feel like a friend has adjusted in a negative way or become distant, pray and ask God how to support her as a friend or simply ask God if it might be time to let go. Not all friendships will remain close throughout your life, and it's okay to have friendships for seasons. No matter the outcome, write down several ways you are thankful for your friend. God gives us the people we need at the right time, and we can thank him for that! Every friend has value in our lives.

## Speak it. Doodle it. Write it out.

A friend loves at all times.
—Proverbs 17:17

## Say a prayer.

*Jesus, please help me be a good friend when my relationships change. I want to listen, care for, and nourish my friendships at all times, even when it's difficult. Amen.*

# DAY 25

# Candid Conversations

When a friendship has come to a confusing patch, there is an option that any loving person can attempt in order to help restore the peace. The Bible tells us, "As iron sharpens iron, so one person sharpens another" (Proverbs 27:17).

This means a good friend will bring clarity and positive challenge to you, and you can do the same for them. You want to have friends who sharpen you like iron. Because as you two talk, share, look into God's Word, and have open conversations, you will become better, smarter, and healthier. A community of honest friendships is a gift from God. The closest of friends check on you and support you so you can be the best you can be. They care for you if you are hurting or not acting like yourself and will try to genuinely listen to your heart.

Processing new situations and circumstances can feel intimidating. At some point, we all deal with shame, nervousness, or uncertainty. So, if you find yourself in a situation where a friend might not be acting like herself, this is the perfect time to gently speak up and ask your friend how she is doing. You can see if anything is new at school, ask how things are at home, or ask what God is doing in her life. It may be uncomfortable at first, but it's the right thing to do. Leading with kindness and care is always a good thing, and friends value being seen and known by each other.

**Speak it. Doodle it. Write it out.**

As iron sharpens iron, so one person sharpens another.
—Proverbs 27:17

**Say a prayer.**

*God, thank you for giving me opportunities to grow in friendship. Please help me speak clearly, love well, and be a friend who is honest and kind. Amen.*

## DAY 26

# Letting Go in Friendship

Perhaps you have a friend who seems to have dropped off the face of the planet. You've prayed for her, texted her to check in, or asked her how she's doing in person. And maybe her response was nonexistent.

Being abandoned—either abruptly or gradually—is tough and devastating. The last handful of school years involve so many transitions, and there can be moments when you might even be met by loss. It's okay to feel frustrated or even angry over the break of a friendship.

If it looks like a friendship has come to a pause, trust God in that waiting space. Even if there wasn't a clear reason why, you can know that God sees you and your friend and that he loves you both. If you allow him to work in your heart while there is space between you, you can possibly step back into that relationship at a later time when things have settled down. And if that relationship never comes back around, it may be the opportunity to learn how to let go and grieve.

Some friendships are more like acquaintances while others are close knit. Breaks are always a reminder to choose your friends carefully. God cares, he sees, and he knows what you need in a true friend. Take a minute to sit, pray, and remind yourself of his faithfulness to you.

### Speak it. Doodle it. Write it out.

The righteous choose their friends carefully, but the
way of the wicked leads them astray.
—Proverbs 12:26

### Say a prayer.

*Jesus, you are the best friend I can have. When other friendships go through struggles or trials, I know that I can always count on you. Thank you for loving me and bringing me peace as I try to be a good friend to others. Amen.*

# DAY 27

# What Do You Mean?

Ever get one of those texts on your phone that leaves you wondering "Is she mad?" Sometimes the most confusing thing in the world is a vague text.

"K"
"Fine"
"No"
"Bye"

When you send a message, it can be received completely different from how you meant it. You might come across annoyed, bothered, or even upset. Or maybe you *are* annoyed, bothered, and upset—and sending a text was a way to avoid eye contact and a hard conversation. No matter what, texting important conversations can always be risky.

Texting can be a great resource for a light conversation or quick response, but it can also cause confusion quickly. Because much of communication comes from what a person doesn't say—tone of voice and body language—texting conversations can make the person receiving the message read more into the words than intended. If you have something serious you need to say, it's always a good idea to see the person in real life or at least hear a tone of voice over the phone.

Overall, we've all had texting go badly in the matter of a few minutes, so we can all remind ourselves today to be gentle, clear, and simple with our electronic communications.

### Speak it. Doodle it. Write it out.

Let your conversation be always full of grace, seasoned with salt, so that you may know how to answer everyone.
—Colossians 4:6

### Say a prayer.

*Jesus, help me be clear in online communications and brave in real conversations. Please remind me to take the opportunities to speak in real life and connect with others through words and actions. Amen.*

# DAY 28

# Wait a Minute

"Ding!"
Less than one minute later . . . "Ding!"
There is a text on the phone. And if you don't answer it in the next sixty seconds, it will remind you with another ding. And as you are eagerly looking for your phone or trying to focus on the task in front of you, you are now thinking about who that text is from and what it says.

This is the plight we live with. Because of phones, we all seem to be accessible to anyone at any time. But it doesn't have to be that way! We can make choices as to when we look at our phones and when we read or respond to text messages. The world will not end if we wait, and we are perfectly allowed to give ourselves breaks from phones and social media. It's always good to hone our self-control and to learn how to live our lives in a way that honors God and honors our time and energy. Constantly responding to our phones distracts us from the people in front of us who are trying to talk with us, be with us, or do something with us.

While the world makes everything feel like an emergency, waiting is often the best thing we can do. Consider setting time limits with your phone. Assign a special ringtone for your parents. Set automatic do not disturb times. Give yourself a reward if you go two hours after school without your phone. The silence will give your heart peace.

**Speak it. Doodle it. Write it out.**

My times are in your hands; deliver me from the hands
of my enemies, from those who pursue me.
—Psalm 31:15

**Say a prayer.**

*Heavenly Father, please remind me of proper boundaries with my phone and social media. It is easy to be consumed by responding, and I need your guidance on how and when to answer and when to wait. Amen.*

DAY 29

# Working for the Lord

Working can be tough. You might not feel motivated, you may not want to, or you might be plain tired. But work is a God-given gift to us to bring us strength, to bless our minds, and to provide for our needs and some of our wants. Finding the balance of good work and rest serves God and others while also helping ourselves.

Unfortunately, the world often gets work confused with worth, and those two are not the same thing. Working hard and achieving is good for our souls, but our worth comes from God.

When you are at your school, going to practice, or working at a job, always remember that you are working to honor God. When your motivation is to do what he'd want you to do, you will be productive in the right ways and do well for your soul and body. Working for God, while maintaining humility, will give you the joy and internal peace that you deserve. If you start to overextend yourself or work for your worth instead of from his strength, you'll find yourself less fulfilled, exhausted, and burnt out. It's always a good idea to ask yourself why you are serving. What is your motivation for doing what you do? Do you want to be obedient to him? Partner with him? Or are you trying to prove yourself? If you answer with the latter, take a minute to pause and seek his heart for you. Ask him if you're functioning in the way he intended.

### Speak it. Doodle it. Write it out.

Whatever you do, work at it with all your heart, as working for the Lord, not for human masters.
—Colossians 3:23

### Say a prayer.

*Jesus, help me to understand the value of hard work. Please bring corrections where I need it, and encourage me to serve in the way you intend for me. Thank you for loving me while I work with you. Amen.*

# DAY 30

# Live Fully

We've all had days when we've tried and failed. Maybe we were working to get acceptance from someone we admire or who we didn't want to disappoint. It's not bad to want to do well, to accomplish, or to help. But when our desire to help and be a support overrides our desire to do what God asks of us, we can get ourselves into trouble.

We all need to be loved and to love. We all need people in our lives who see us and value us, but the reality is that we can only give out what we have. So, if we are performing out of a need to be accepted, we have little value to give and end up more depleted than when we started. And unfortunately, we are worshiping our acceptance from people more than we are focused on serving others.

When God is first in our lives, his goodness and grace fuel us to function differently. You just might find that when you seek to serve God, he will reward you . . . often in ways you least expect. It's a beautiful flow of receiving from him and then giving away to others. When our friends do the same, it's an example of God's design for support and community. And nothing else is more satisfying than living with God and good friends.

### Speak it. Doodle it. Write it out.

You did not choose me, but I chose you. I appointed you to go and produce fruit and that your fruit should remain, so that whatever you ask the Father in my name, he will give you.
—John 15:16 CSB

### Say a prayer.

*Jesus, you are the best friend there is. Help me to live out of fullness in you, so that I can serve others from the grace you've given me. Amen.*

## DAY 31

# Expectation Troubles

Let's talk about expectations. Expectations can make or break us. Sometimes we go about life expecting something will be given to us or provided for us in a certain way at a certain time. It's not necessarily wrong to want something, but expecting it can lead to entitlement if we aren't careful.

Have you ever thought your parents were going to buy you something, and then they said no? How did you respond? Were you understanding or frustrated? Your answer may depend on your comprehension of the whole situation. You may have expected something that was too much or too big, and you realized after the fact that your expectations weren't fair. But you may have reacted with frustration because you thought they'd promised or it felt like something you needed.

Being left with disappointment can be a bummer, but it also can point us to the truth. The truth is God will always provide what we need, but it might not be what we expected or in the way we anticipated. And that is okay. In fact, it's even good. When we put our trust or hope in something other than God, sometimes it will let us down. But when we align our desires with what Jesus wants, he will always fill us with what is best for us. And ultimately, that is what we want.

### Speak it. Doodle it. Write it out.

"For my thoughts are not your thoughts, and your ways are not my ways." This is the Lord's declaration. "For as heaven is higher than earth, so my ways are higher than your ways, and my thoughts than your thoughts."
—Isaiah 55:8–9 CSB

### Say a prayer.

*God, help me to be clear of unrealistic expectations. Remind me that life is a process, and you are leading me into the best experiences for my journey. Amen.*

# DAY 32

# Think on These Things

Scientific studies show that grumbling or complaining actually tells our minds to look for more bad things. You are what you think! Which means self-pity, self-focus, and a negative attitude can be debilitating. That's why it's always important to see ourselves and the world as God himself sees it. And we can do that by reading his Word. God is perfect, and the Bible is filled with truth which is the cure to the lies of the world.

There are going to be days when your mind is at war. Perhaps you're calculating all the money you don't have, the boy you would like to date, or the clothes you wish you had. Your mind is going on that downward spiral. Our world is not enough, no matter how you look at it. It's fallen and broken, but Jesus is not. He is the perfect fulfillment of all that we love, need, want, and desire. He is the source of all things good.

So, the next time you only see what you don't have or what's wrong, stop. Take a minute to remember all the ways God has provided for you, surprised you, and loved you when you needed it. Write them down, and post them where you can see them each night and morning. Look in his Word and meditate on the promises that he has made to you, knowing that he does come through. And he does fulfill. We simply need to focus on him.

### Speak it. Doodle it. Write it out.

Finally, brothers and sisters, whatever is true, whatever is noble, whatever is right, whatever is pure, whatever is lovely, whatever is admirable—if anything is excellent or praiseworthy—think about such things.
—Philippians 4:8

### Say a prayer.

*Father God, life can be difficult. I want to complain and grumble sometimes. Help me think on all that you have done and be grateful for my circumstances. Amen.*

## DAY 33

# Quality over Quantity

Have you ever eaten too much ice cream? Sometimes getting that large sundae with all the toppings tastes good going down the hatch but later leaves you bloated and gurgling.

In a lot of ways, the world can be like that enormous dessert—full of glitz and glitter, with shiny things, and delicious treats. Yet too much of a good thing can be bad. Knowing when to treat yourself and also when to stop is a life lesson everyone can benefit from. A few bites of delicious ice cream can be enough of a treat to enjoy the gift God gave you without losing self-control which binds you into indigestion regret. Choosing to celebrate the quality of something—whether ice cream, friendships, clothing, or time—over choosing the quantity of it can be essential. More isn't also better, and finding the value in restraint can help us stay away from gluttony and greed.

The next time you have a choice between quality over quantity, think through your decision. How much is that ice cream worth? That pair of jeans? Being popular? Is it worth the time, energy, and cost to recover yourself? Simplicity can be freeing, and loading on too much of a good thing can weigh you down.

### Speak it. Doodle it. Write it out.

And I pray this: that your love will keep on growing in knowledge and every kind of discernment, so that you may approve the things that are superior and may be pure and blameless in the day of Christ.
—Philippians 1:9–10 CSB

### Say a prayer.

*Holy Spirit, please help me receive self-control from you. I want to make healthy choices that are wise and fruitful. Remind me that more is not always better. Amen.*

# DAY 34

# He's Cute

Perhaps he has the same lunch hour as you. Or maybe he goes to your youth group. He could live in your neighborhood, or maybe he's a family friend.

Whoever he is, he caught your eye. Perhaps he even made your heart flutter a little bit, or you felt butterflies in your belly when you saw him. You might get nervous if you talk to him, and all these feelings point to the fact that you may officially have a crush.

It's completely normal to have an interest in someone who may or may not feel the same way about you. And it can feel complicated. It can take up all your thoughts, rolling around in your brain and heart, keeping you awake at night, and making you daydream during class. The teenage years are full of crushes, first loves, and sometimes even future husbands.

Liking a boy is part of growing up. It's wonderful to want to experience a dating relationship. Though it's nothing to be ashamed of, it can bring about feelings of embarrassment, rejection, or even fear. But you deserve the best, so don't settle for anything less! Over the next few days, we'll dig into Jesus's guidance and talk through a few things to expect when it comes to growing in relationships.

### Speak it. Doodle it. Write it out.

Take delight in the LORD, and he will give you the desires of your heart.
—Psalm 37:4

### Say a prayer.

*Jesus, please guide me in this time of transition with relationships. Help me to know what is good and right. Please show me how you have designed my life for dating relationships in this season. Amen.*

DAY 35

# Needs of the Heart

Does he like me? He might act like he crushes on you one day and ignore you the next. He might pick on you, flirt with you, and then do the same with another girl who is in your class. Boys can be tricky to navigate. Sometimes they do have crushes, and sometimes they just have changing hormones. The mind games might make you feel a little crazy.

There are a lot of things to consider when you have those initial feelings of interest. And let me tell you, you aren't alone! Mulling through a crush and wondering if he feels the same can take up a lot of your energy and can really yank on your heartstrings.

I could have saved some time and heartache by sitting down with God and asking him what my life truly needed. If I'd done that more intentionally, I would have received some answers that would have given me clarity and a deeper confidence in myself. My hope is that I can shed some of that light for you, so that you will have plenty to think about and pray through as you learn how to grow in confidence and watch God meet your needs with himself. He might also bring a relationship into your life to help you grow and learn, and that will be up to you and your parents. Let's start this conversation about the needs of the heart with a prayer today.

### Speak it. Doodle it. Write it out.

*But seek first the kingdom of God and his righteousness, and all these things will be provided for you.*
—Matthew 6:33 CSB

### Say a prayer.

*Jesus, there is a lot going on in my heart. My life is transforming and changing and so are the lives of my peers, including potential boyfriends. Help me to hear from you clearly during this season of life. Help me to know my needs are met by you and instill a deep confidence in me. Amen.*

# DAY 36

# Speak Up

Maybe he keeps coming around, and he is flirting and making an effort to be by you, but he hasn't asked you on a date or said a thing about it. Let me tell you, I've been there! Here are a few possible reasons why he's not taking the next step:

Sometimes boys are nervous to ask a girl out. You might say no, and no one likes rejection.

Sometimes boys aren't looking for a serious relationship, and they're just having fun as friends. Girls can read more into a friendship romantically when boys are simply just enjoying the time together. Confusing, right?

Sometimes girls need to be the brave one and gently ask, "Are we just friends? Or is something more going on here?" It doesn't hurt to clear the air . . . as long as we're kind. Otherwise, the confusing uncertainty could go on for months and months. If he says you're just friends, then take a deep breath, and let that sink in. If he says he wants to be more than that, think that over and decide what the next steps might be. Waiting too long to ask can create confusion in the relationship, and it might lead to a longer heartache. Being honest is a good way to show your integrity and strength. No matter what happens, speaking up will serve you in the long run and in a relationship of any kind.

### Speak it. Doodle it. Write it out.

My words come from my upright heart, and my lips
speak with sincerity what they know.
—Job 33:3 CSB

### Say a prayer.

*Jesus, please help me to be honest with my thoughts and feelings. I ask for bravery and kindness as I speak up for myself and allow my heart to be known. Amen.*

# DAY 37

# It's a Date

Perhaps it is a mutual crush. What next? Well, first things first, what do your parents say about dating? What are the rules? Are you allowed to be in a relationship yet? If so, then perhaps you can slowly start to move forward and try a few dates together. If not, please respect your parents' rules.

Let me repeat, respect your parents' rules!

With no beating around the bush, here's why: if you don't respect your parents' decision, it will only cause issues between you and your mom and dad. That doesn't mean you shouldn't bring up the fact that you like someone. That's not wrong at all. You are a young woman, and it's only natural to start wanting to pursue a dating relationship. But the feedback your parents give you about that dating relationship is extremely important. You may be surprised. Asking for your parents' thoughts on a certain boy may actually open up the possibility of them considering him. But if they say no, going behind their back won't help. Doing what you want, outside of their approval, will make them lose trust in you. And that will hinder future communication when discussing boyfriends at another time.

So, take it step by step here. Find out what each of your parents' expectations are in regard to you dating, and be clear and honest from the beginning. If everyone is on the same page, it's a wonderful opportunity to consider how to move forward now and in the future.

**Speak it. Doodle it. Write it out.**

Honor your father and mother, which is the first commandment with a promise, so that it may go well with you and that you may have a long life in the land.
—Ephesians 6:2–3 CSB

**Say a prayer.**

*Jesus, help me to respect and listen to my parents about dating relationships. Open my ears to hear wisdom and to be smart in my decisions about how to move forward when my feelings might want to run the show. Amen.*

# DAY 38

# It's Official

Let's say that all parents say "yes" to moving forward with this dating relationship. Exciting, right? What do you do next? What does it look like to have a boyfriend or a guy friend?

Every relationship will look a little different. Maybe it will start simple with after-school hangouts at sporting events or in the neighborhood, or maybe you're a bit older and driving on a date is included. Relationships allow us to enjoy one another and learn more about him through people who are dedicated to us in a deeper way. This is a season of growth, integrity, and fun whether you stay in a group of friends or go to a dinner date one-on-one.

New relationships are valuable and help us learn. The decisions you make today will affect your life long term, and it's wise to stay open in communication with older people you trust, those who can walk with you a bit through these transitions. How do you feel after hanging out with your boyfriend? Does he ask good questions and want to hear your thoughts? Does he encourage you to be a good person?

Have fun, enjoy life and all its seasons, and be smart! Though it's easy to get caught up in the buzz of relationships at this stage, this is just the beginning of where God will lead you. Take things slow, and pray along the way. God will give you courage and grace as you navigate the newness of dating relationships.

### Speak it. Doodle it. Write it out.

The boundary lines have fallen for me in pleasant places; surely I have a delightful inheritance.
—Psalm 16:6

### Say a prayer.

*Holy Spirit, you are wise and smart and counsel me well. Thank you for guiding me with peace and joy, for helping me learn the ways of life and love. Amen.*

# DAY 39

# Breathe and Pray

Anxiety has been at the forefront of news for the last several years. Everyone knows how it feels at one time or another, some of us more than others. Your heart races, your face feels tingly. You might even feel panic or anger rise as you're overwhelmed by thoughts and your mind traces outcomes at a million miles a minute. Your senses are on overload, and it's extremely uncomfortable. Whether it's stress from school, friendships, or family life, or whether your hormones are running the show, it can feel at times like there is no rest for all the thoughts and worries in your head. So what do you do with the anxiety that grips you or the fear that wants to run your life?

Breathing deeply is always a great start because worries love to steal your air and wrap your chest in knots. But just taking deep breaths isn't enough to cure what ails us. The Bible says to "cast all your anxiety on him because he cares for you."

That might seem easier said than done, but sitting down with God to talk it out surely does help. The Creator of the universe wants to be in a close relationship with you. You can rest assured that you can tell him anything and know he's listening. Try it. Sometimes just knowing that we're heard can shift anxiety right out of our hearts.

### Speak it. Doodle it. Write it out.

Cast all your anxiety on him because he cares for you.
—1 Peter 5:7

### Say a prayer.

*Holy Spirit, I ask for your comfort. Give me your breath and your peace, allowing me to let go of my hurts, fears, anxieties, and worries. Amen.*

# DAY 40

# Healthy Choices Win

Worries often come to your mind because of emotional stress. But do you know what else can cause the jitters? Not enough good nutrients or insufficient sleep. At times, when you feel those worries increase or that fear start to rise, ask yourself when you ate last or if you've had a vitamin that day or how much water you've drank. With all the opportunities to consume sugar, energy drinks, and coffee these days, it can be a real challenge to intake the proper fuel for your body's needs.

Unfortunately, coffee isn't a full form of nutrition, even though it gives our body a form of energy. And when that coffee bean has set your mind awake, it can also make your heart and body shake. We need adequate forms of protein and carbohydrates to fuel our daily lives. If you haven't added something green to your diet, consider doing that several times a week for a natural, earthy source of nutrition. And, of course, sleep! Sleeping helps our body and mind repair themselves.

So before letting that worry get you down, consider the last time you had some protein. Grab a sandwich or eat a burger, take a nap, and then see if your worries calm down on their own.

## Speak it. Doodle it. Write it out.

So whether you eat or drink or whatever you do, do it all for the glory of God.
—1 Corinthians 10:31

## Say a prayer.

*Jesus, you are the Prince of Peace, and you also are the Bread of Life. Remind me to fill up spiritually from your Word and also to fill up physically with healthy food. Amen.*

# DAY 41

# Be Kind to Yourself

Life is full of choices and opportunities. It's full of mistakes and jobs well done. Some days you will feel great about yourself and other days, you might feel like the worst person ever. No matter what the day is like, it's always a good day to be kind to yourself.

Maybe someone taught you the Bible in a way that made kindness for yourself difficult. Perhaps punishing and avoiding sin was always front and center, but the kindness that leads to the repentance of that sin wasn't really offered. Because of that, shame or self-hatred took root and self-blame became present instead of allowing the Holy Spirit to gently convict and offer forgiveness and restoration. There's a difference between knowing we did wrong and verbally abusing ourselves for doing wrong. We need the kindness of Christ to change. We cannot do it on our own.

You'll have plenty of opportunities to do the right thing throughout your life. There will also be plenty of times that you'll make a mistake. The beauty of living a life with Jesus is that he is always patient and kind to us as we journey here on earth. If you're seeking God, he will not strike you down and neither should anyone else . . . including you. Perhaps today is a day you need to be warm and gentle with yourself. Treat yourself to a small act of self-care today. Jesus loves you and is with you through it all.

### Speak it. Doodle it. Write it out.

Or do you despise the riches of his kindness, restraint, and patience, not recognizing that God's kindness is intended to lead you to repentance?
—Romans 2:4 CSB

### Say a prayer.

*Jesus, thank you for your grace as I navigate my life. You are loving and kind, careful and corrective. Help me to remember to take it all one step at a time. Amen.*

## DAY 42

# Honesty Brings Connection

"Can I be honest?"

That's often a question we ask when we want to tell someone the truth without hurting their feelings or having our feelings hurt. We might be nervous about telling the truth. It might make us feel vulnerable or open to rejection.

Yet Jesus was a truth teller. All throughout the Gospels, he was very honest with people who were struggling, who needed healing, and who wanted him in their life. He wanted them to speak and receive honesty because they could then receive his goodness and his guidance. The essence of forgiveness is the ability to admit the truth and ask Jesus to transform us in our shortcomings. If we aren't honest, then we don't actually connect with and know one another. This also means we don't get to connect with or know Jesus more.

The world often uses screens to hide from true relationships. As a result, it can seem easier to isolate or type from far away than to talk face-to-face. But Scripture says sharing our struggles and sins is how Jesus turns on the metaphorical light for us when we are hidden in the dark. By being authentic and then praying with one another for God's help, we often see real-life changes happen like growth in friendships and a deeper understanding of God's grace. So today, turn off your phone and have a real conversation with a friend or family member.

### Speak it. Doodle it. Write it out.

For where two or three gather together as my followers, I am there among them.
—Matthew 18:20 NLT

### Say a prayer.

*Jesus, help me to be honest and brave. Give me kind words to speak while also telling the truth in a way that communicates grace and love. Amen.*

# DAY 43

# Will You Still Love Me?

Your math test came back with a big red D on it. First, you gasp, Then, you panic. You know that you didn't study very well. You're embarrassed and ashamed.

Or . . .

Your math test came back with a big red D on it. First, you gasp. Then, you panic. You tried as hard as you could, and you still didn't make the grade you hoped for. What a disappointment.

These are two different scenarios, but they are both real possibilities. Sometimes our results match our efforts, and sometimes our results don't at all line up with our efforts. No matter the case, God still loves us the same. God is faithful, and he loves us eternally, unconditionally, and with no exceptions. When we fail to do our work, we likely won't see positive results. All of our decisions, whether good or bad, do result in a consequence.

However, sometimes we will do the work with the best effort we can give, and we still won't see the results we hoped for. It is okay not to be a perfect student (or human). We can panic ourselves into performance and then realize that performing perfectly isn't what God requires of us.

Though God always encourages valid effort and diligence, his opinion of us never changes. Write down the words of Lamentations 3:22–23 today, and remember how God loves you!

**Speak it. Doodle it. Write it out.**

Because of the Lord's great love we are not consumed, for his compassions never fail. They are new every morning; great is your faithfulness.
—Lamentations 3:22–23

**Say a prayer.**

*God, thank you for loving me no matter how I perform. Your care for me is not based on how well I do or how right I am. You love me because I am yours. Thank you. Amen.*

# DAY 44

# Which Path?

Ever have a decision to make and it feels like the weight of the world is on your shoulders? Sometimes decisions can feel that way, like tugging between two opposite choices or even between two good choices. Life is full of opportunities, and choosing your path should come with prayer and thought.

Looking in the Word for help when making a decision is a great place to start! You can find encouraging words, helpful prayers, and examples of people who went through similar situations. If you need a little guidance for where to find those resources in Scripture, ask a parent, pastor, or mentor in your life for direction. Though the Bible is a large book and may feel intimidating, there are many tools to help you find what you're looking for. You may even ask your mentors about using a concordance, which helps you look up specific words and stories.

When you find a verse or passage that seems like it might address your concerns, spend time praying and carefully reading through that Scripture. It's okay if your decision isn't clear right away. Let God lead you through his words as you do and then take steps on the path he is showing you. You will find both faith and joy in the process, and you can walk forward without fear.

## Speak it. Doodle it. Write it out.

Your word is a lamp for my feet, a light on my path.
—Psalm 119:105

## Say a prayer.

*Heavenly Father, guide me in your Word. Make your light and life come alive on the pages. I want to live in sync with your Scriptures and truth. Amen.*

# DAY 45

# Hormone Messages

Hormones. Those chemical messengers running through your body telling you that today might be the worst day ever in the history of evers. They start flowing, and your belly starts bloating. Your exhaustion sets in, and it's all a fatigue-filled blur from there. And every woman knows it.

But hormones don't have to ruin your day. The good news is that, despite making you feel grouchy and slouchy, your chemical messengers help your body grow and transform into a woman, preparing you for the ability to nurture life and regulating your internal balance of temperature and electrolytes. The tough thing is that they can also make you feel emotional with an attitude to boot, and they can contribute to grouchiness and slouchiness.

When the roller-coaster feelings come to the surface, causing anxiety and sadness, remind yourself that God designed you perfectly. And in those moments of uncomfortable meltdowns, he is with you even then. Take the time to rest your body, recalibrate your soul, and give yourself the grace to be at peace with yourself and all your femaleness.

The reality is that hormones will come and go throughout your life. And they often come as a surprise, but knowing that God included them as part of his creation gives you a purpose to walk through them (walking literally helps) with peace and calm. It's good to be a girl, even when it's tough!

### Speak it. Doodle it. Write it out.

So God created mankind in his own image, in the image of God he created them; male and female he created them.
—Genesis 1:27

### Say a prayer.

*God, thank you for designing my body intentionally. Thank you for your choice to make me a girl. Help me honor my body with rest and recovery through all of its transitions and changes. Amen.*

DAY 46

# Do Not Be Afraid

Anxiety can be debilitating. It can ruin the course of your day and keep you from reaching the potential that is inside you. Anxious feelings or thoughts can be rooted in fear or they can be neurological at their core. Many times our environments are loud and overstimulating, which can also make our bodies imbalanced. When not in balance, we can feel jittery, on edge, and fearful.

Many people in Scripture struggled with fear in different forms, and the most common command in the Bible is, "Do not be afraid." Repeating it around three hundred times, God must really want us not to be afraid. But even when we know our peace is important to God, we still might struggle to set aside anxiety and put our faith into motion.

And that's why we practice prayer. Just like you lift heavy weights to gain muscle and bring your body stability, you also can pray to calm your anxious thoughts and feelings. Taking a deep breath and speaking out loud is especially effective. Let's try it now. Inhale from deep in your core and then exhale while whispering "Jesus" several times in a row. Inhale again. Then speak the verse at the end of this devotion. As you hear your voice speak about God's love and comfort, his strength and courage, your body and mind begin to believe you. With time and practice, your fear will start to diminish. Try it the next time you feel anxiety start to rise, and repeat it as often as necessary.*

---

\* If your anxiety feels overwhelming, it might be due to a deeper issue like a neurological condition or chemical imbalance. Talk to a trusted adult, such as a parent or school counselor, or reach out to a professional for support. If you need immediate help, you can also call or text 988, the national Suicide & Crisis Lifeline.

### Speak it. Doodle it. Write it out.

Have I not commanded you? Be strong and courageous. Do not be afraid; do not be discouraged, for the LORD your God will be with you wherever you go.
—Joshua 1:9

### Say a prayer.

*Jesus, help me with my anxiety. When I get stuck and don't know how to move forward, remind me to take small steps toward you in prayer and action. Thank you for calming my fears. Amen.*

# DAY 47

# Fear of Missing Out

In a world that changes every single day, we all can struggle to keep up. Because of the FOMO, we trade what we actually need for the opinions of others. This not only doesn't help us, but it can move us in the wrong direction by placing us in distracting company. It can change us in ways God doesn't intend for us. It's like choosing to hang out with a questionable group of new friends when you have a test to study for the following day. Making the right decision is important.

The reality is life is always transitioning, and we will have to decide what and who are worth running after and what and who aren't. Just because the majority of people are doing something doesn't mean that it's right, and being firm in our convictions and beliefs helps us not be swayed by the options presented by others. It might sometimes feel like life moves on without you, and it's actually okay if you let it.

The teenage years are a constant source of change, but you can always remember one thing: Jesus doesn't change. *He is the same yesterday, today, and forever.* Write that on your journal page or in your notebook. Make it bold by layering each letter. Jesus is faithful to love us and stand by us. Abide in his Word and in his peace as you doodle.

### Speak it. Doodle it. Write it out.

Jesus Christ is the same yesterday and today and forever.
—Hebrews 13:8

### Say a prayer.

*Jesus, thank you for your faithfulness to me. When everything around me is changing and moving, help me to find my peace in you. I want to trust in your plans and purposes. Amen.*

DAY 48

# Ask for Help

Life can feel somewhat lonely, especially when we could use a bit of help. Sometimes we avoid asking for support because we're embarrassed or intimidated. What if someone will think less of us if we have a sin that we are struggling with? Or what if we don't have enough money to afford something that is essential? What if we've asked for help previously, and no one had the time? Whatever the case, not only is it okay to be struggling, asking for help is a good thing to do.

God created us to live in a community so that we could share with each other. We need one another to help shed light on our darkness, to share wisdom in our struggles, and to practically share resources. Christian community is in your life to support and love you, whether you are tangled up in a mess of mistakes or struggling to make sense of your circumstances. In fact, the Bible calls us to share our burdens with one another, to confess our sins to each other, and to help those in need.

So the next time you may feel too vulnerable to be authentic and real, take a moment to find a friend who loves you and cares for you, and talk it out. Perhaps meet in a small group weekly or monthly where healthy relationships can grow. When we pray together and help each other, we find our purpose and goals together.

### Speak it. Doodle it. Write it out.

And let us consider how we may spur one another on toward love and good deeds, not giving up meeting together, as some are in the habit of doing, but encouraging one another—and all the more as you see the Day approaching.
—Hebrews 10:24–25

### Say a prayer.

*Jesus, thank you for friends who love you and who love me. Help me to be open and honest in my relationships and to ask for support when I need it. Amen.*

# DAY 49

# Burnt Out?

Have you ever reached to turn on a light and instead of flicking on, it just burns out? A quick sizzle occurs and then . . . nothing. People can be that way too. If we have done all that we can do and have burned brightly on all our cylinders, sometimes we blow a fuse. Living life fully requires rest. Schoolwork, extracurriculars, and jobs can make us busy, and commitments require a lot of our time, energy, and effort.

Maybe you're a leader at your school or activity and so you feel the constant tug of helping others in addition to helping yourself. Or perhaps you are struggling with schoolwork, and no matter how hard you try, you just don't get it. The responsibility and the pressure can take a toll on you, and if you aren't careful, you'll likely end up with an abrupt stop like an injury or even sickness. While you are living your best life or trying to manage your current circumstance, make sure you also take the time to care for yourself, eat well, and get enough rest. Reminding yourself that you can say no to things, even if you are good at them, can help you to stay within proper boundaries.

Consider setting an alarm on your phone in two-hour increments. Take a few sips of water each time it goes off, pray for God's peace and wisdom to be with you as you go on with your day, and thank God for his protection.

## Speak it. Doodle it. Write it out.

Come to me, all you who are weary and burdened, and I will give you rest. Take my yoke upon you and learn from me, for I am gentle and humble in heart, and you will find rest for your souls. For my yoke is easy and my burden is light.
—Matthew 11:28–30

## Say a prayer.

*Jesus, thank you for allowing me to use my gifts and work hard. Help me to maintain my peace while serving, and please give me seasons of rest to balance out the seasons of busy. Amen.*

# DAY 50

# Nothing Is Impossible

Challenges. Dreams. Possibilities.

Those three words go together when you desire to change the world. Life is full of hope, and God may ask you to do something impossible. Yes, I said impossible! You may feel like an average teenager with not a lot to offer, but God does not see you that way.

Do you realize that the parents of Jesus were likely right around the same age you are currently? That in itself speaks to the fact that God values teens and their contributions, especially since he used a teenager to shift the entire course of humanity by birthing the Savior of the world. Thank goodness that Jesus leads us and goes with us as we embark on changing the world around us. He is the possible in a situation that seems impossible.

In fact, the mother of Jesus was a young girl who was visited by an angel to foretell of his birth. She was not married and had not even been intimate before. Can you imagine what she must have felt and thought? Write down a few of her possible feelings. And even in the midst of her overwhelm, God was with her while she transformed history just by saying "yes" to him. Jesus was then born into a lowly and humble situation, in a manger with animals and little else. Do you have a seemingly impossible goal or circumstance in your life? How can you let go of your fear or unbelief today, and let God do the seemingly impossible through you? Raise your hands with palms up, surrender your worries to God, and ask to receive the grace you need to overcome.

### Speak it. Doodle it. Write it out.

But the angel said to her, "Do not be afraid, Mary; you have found favor with God."
—Luke 1:30

### Say a prayer.

*Jesus, thank you for being with me on the overwhelmingly difficult days. Help me receive your presence into my day and circumstances, so that I can partner with you to achieve what seems impossible. Amen.*

# DAY 51

# Respect Elders

I live in the South where most adults are met by "Yes, ma'am" and "Yes, sir." That might seem foreign to you where you live, but maybe you call adults by terms like Mr. or Mrs.

Wherever you live, speaking to adults with respect is important. Not only have they lived a lot longer than you, most adults want what's best for you. If you are part of a church or team, you likely have adults around you who encourage you and help guide you to what is good and right. That doesn't mean you'll always like what they suggest for you, but their experience plus their care means that it's a good idea to listen.

At times, we all want to rebel or do the opposite of what authority says. It's normal to ask questions and push against boundaries when we're trying to find our footing, but what you don't want to do is sass back, roll your eyes, or think you know it all. Why? God asks us to respect those in authority because it prevents chaos, because honor for one another keeps us healthy, and because humility leads to favor. In the long run, it's always smarter to listen to a healthy adult's suggestions and guidance for your life. Who do you have in your life that you can trust? How can you show that person honor and respect today?

### Speak it. Doodle it. Write it out.

In the same way, you who are younger, submit yourselves to your elders. All of you, clothe yourselves with humility toward one another, because, "God opposes the proud but shows favor to the humble."
—1 Peter 5:5

### Say a prayer.

*Jesus, thank you for the adults in my life who love me and have my best interests at heart. Help me to be a good listener and to respect those who care for me. Amen.*

# DAY 52

# Mentoring Guides

Having mentors and coaches in your life you can learn from is a big bonus! Do you go to youth group or meet with someone a little bit older who can encourage you in your faith? It's a great idea to do that if you already aren't. You wouldn't set out on an unfamiliar wilderness trail on your own, right? No way! And life can often feel like an unfamiliar wilderness trail.

Learning from someone older than you is like having an experienced trail guide for all those tree roots, puddles, and drop-offs. A guide could give you insight into what you might expect as you go through the next few years. Kind of like reading this devotional, a mentor can give you tips and ideas to help you get the most out of this season of life. And they'll also be able to help lead and encourage you when you hit hard situations or circumstances.

Being a teen isn't always easy. There's a lot of pressure from other kids as well as from social media and TV. Asking a trusted friend questions about her experience as a teenager helps lessen the load. Most older friends love sharing and being able to listen to you while you sort through your challenges and joys. Think about a few older friends from youth group, work, or school. Consider asking one of them to meet with you every month to encourage you in this season.

### Speak it. Doodle it. Write it out.

Follow my example, as I follow the example of Christ.
—1 Corinthians 11:1

### Say a prayer.

*Jesus, thank you for the youth leaders and mentors in my life. Would you give me time to sit down and listen to their advice, pray with them, and be encouraged by them? Amen.*

# DAY 53

# Speaking Well

I'm sure you've heard a lot of swearing or angry words after school, in the mall, or around town, maybe even in your own home. You don't have to go far to hear things that are crass, rude, inappropriate, or just downright mean. Unfortunately, there is a lot of hurt in the world, and Jesus says how people speak is often an example of what's in their hearts. What we say is powerful. Whether good or bad, our words and our emotions affect those around us.

There are a lot of reasons we can slip into using ugly language. One of the biggest is when we're angry or frustrated. In those situations, we might struggle to take time to think before we speak. Lashing out is sometimes easier than taking a breath. But if you take self-controlled pauses, God can reveal better ways to express yourself. Soothing anger with deep breaths, pauses, and prayer can completely turn around a negative situation.

People may speak insensitively to look cool or impress others even without an angry undertone, but no matter what, ugly language is hurtful and abusive. Jesus calls us to speak words that are kind and encouraging. Instead of speaking crass and unkind words, pause and take a breath. Let go of unresolved anger, and find a way to say what might need saying with kindness and gentleness. If you struggle with your words, write the phrase "speak life" on your hand to remind you to slow down.

### Speak it. Doodle it. Write it out.

A good man brings good things out of the good stored up in his heart, and an evil man brings evil things out of the evil stored up in his heart. For the mouth speaks what the heart is full of.
—Luke 6:45

### Say a prayer.

*Jesus, help me to keep a guard over my mouth and self-control in my heart. Please heal me of wounds that would cause me to speak unkindly or hurtfully. Amen.*

## DAY 54

# Goals and Dreams

Ever had a dream burning in your heart that you felt like you just had to accomplish? Maybe it's getting a part in a play or participating in an elite club sport. Perhaps you would like to write a book someday or serve in a country that could use a few extra helping hands. Goals and dreams are good to have! They bring hope, motion, and life to our bones. It's good to want to do good, and there are a lot of ways to accomplish it.

If you have a dream or goal in your heart, what is it? What can you do to get started? Most of the time, goals don't happen overnight but take a lot of little steps each day. At times, you might experience setbacks, it might seem difficult, and it can even feel impossible. That's okay. These tough days build perseverance, and they fuel you to seek God for help through prayer. Other days, you might feel like the wind is in your sails, and you get a lot done with little effort. Take the opportunity to thank God and express gratitude for all the ways he gives you grace for your journey.

Think through some of the ideas and dreams of your heart, and give them to God. Ask him how you can get moving, and enjoy the process! God loves doing more for us than we can ever think or imagine. And participating with him is the best!

### Speak it. Doodle it. Write it out.

Now to him who is able to do immeasurably more than all we ask or imagine, according to his power that is at work within us, to him be glory in the church and in Christ Jesus throughout all generations, for ever and ever! Amen.
—Ephesians 3:20–21

### Say a prayer.

*Heavenly Father, I give you my goals and dreams, my hopes and future accomplishments. Will you help me serve you? Open my eyes to see the next steps you have for me. Amen.*

# DAY 55

# Sibling Love

Do you have any brothers or sisters? Siblings are a blessing, but they can also be a little tough to deal with. Maybe you are close with your siblings, or maybe you don't talk much. Perhaps your brother or sister really rubs you the wrong way, and you get in fights a lot. Even if you and your siblings are close, you'll still get in an argument every once in a while because, well, you're human. Whether you have siblings or whether you're an only child, living your day-to-day life with other people teaches you a lot about how to live like Jesus.

The people we live closest to get the real-life view of us—in our pajamas, or when we wake up, or when we are sick—and that means they often know us the best. And those are the people we can serve every day, whether on purpose or just because we share a house with them. The next time a brother or sister irritates you, or copies you, or takes your turn in the bathroom, just remember that loving them well will be one of the best things you do in life because you will always hold a family bond. Try jotting down a list of your favorite things about each brother or sister. Hang onto that list for when they irritate you. Remembering why you love him or her will help you smile and be patient as you live each day together.

### Speak it. Doodle it. Write it out.

So, my brothers and sisters, you also died to the law through the body of Christ, that you might belong to another, to him who was raised from the dead, in order that we might bear fruit for God.
—Romans 7:4

### Say a prayer.

*God, thank you for siblings to live with and love. Help me to be a kind, caring, and forgiving sister. Amen.*

# DAY 56

# Sleeping Sorrows

Tossing. Turning. Thinking. Overthinking. Thinking again. Worrying. Counting sheep. It's the worst. When you can't fall asleep or you're up all night filled with anxiety or tomorrow's worries, you'll not only be groggy the next day but also struggle with finding the joy of rest and peace.

There are a lot of reasons why you might toss and turn at night. Maybe it's a big test the next day, or you had an argument with a friend, perhaps it's a boy you're thinking about, or maybe you disappointed a parent with your behavior or attitude. Sometimes we don't sleep because we are full of concerns. And when that happens, it's important to remember one thing: God never slumbers or sleeps. In fact, the Bible says: "He will not let your foot slip—he who watches over you will not slumber; indeed, he who watches over Israel will neither slumber nor sleep."

So, the next time you're tossing and turning, remember that God isn't. He doesn't sleep and he doesn't panic. Instead, he is calmly watching over you. Memorize Psalm 121: 3–4 and speak it over yourself each night. Rest assured that you can take a few deep breaths, give your worries to him, and he will take care of you.

**Speak it. Doodle it. Write it out.**

He will not let your foot slip—he who watches over you will not slumber;
indeed, he who watches over Israel will neither slumber nor sleep.
—Psalm 121:3–4

**Say a prayer.**

*Father God, sometimes worries consume me, and I need your help to rest. Remind me of your watchful heart, and help me let go of whatever I'm holding on to. Amen.*

# DAY 57

# No One Better

You're going to have a lot of decisions to make over the next few years. What to wear, who to hang out with, what to believe. Culture and society have a lot to say about your freedoms as a person, and they approve of many things as okay that the Bible actually says are not okay.

At times, you will be faced with people who challenge your beliefs. That can be a good thing because it can make you stronger in knowing the truth, or it can be a bad thing if those people sway you away from Jesus. Jesus doesn't have an ego complex to constantly be right, be the winner, or one-up others. Jesus actually is "the way and the truth and the life" (John 14:6). Everything we do and say should lead to him because he himself is the truth.

Did you know Jesus is the only religious leader who died intentionally for the people he loves? He gave up his perfect existence to be beaten, mocked, and judged in order to save us from everything we have ever done wrong. Then he rose from the dead and is preparing an even better place for us to live forever. Stop and think about that. Your debt is paid, canceled, taken away forever.

No other god or opinion in the world has done that. Doodle the word "best" on your notebook, or make a bead bracelet where the letters spell out "best." Thank Jesus for officially being the best.

## Speak it. Doodle it. Write it out.

"To whom will you compare me? Or who is my equal?" says the Holy One.
—Isaiah 40:25

## Say a prayer.

*Jesus, thank you for what you've done for me. Help me to live my life in a way that honors what you have done. Make my heart steadfast to love you. Amen.*

# DAY 58

# Be a Peacemaker

Disagreements are a normal part of life. Each person has his or her own life experiences and views, and there will be times when those views collide with their friends'. It's good to remember that making peace is always an important part in helping everyone feel valued and heard.

Living as a peacemaker is one of God's instructions to us, and one of Jesus's names is Prince of Peace. Jesus was born into a chaotic world to transform our lives from sin to true life. Being Christians, we get to follow in his footsteps by bringing his peace to others.

What does that look like in your everyday life? Encouraging a friend? Praying for someone who is struggling? Listening to someone who needs a voice? Helping someone forgive and let go? Purposely supporting others to live in peace and find calm will also help you go far in life and in your relationships. It's difficult to work with and be friends with those who are constantly causing drama or making others feel bad about themselves. It is uncomfortable and makes our minds and bodies irritable.

You can do the opposite! Bring people together to hear one another gently, and practice listening to each other. Stand up for what is right by being a person who loves others well. Send a friend an encouraging handwritten note or a text this week. Be a person of peace to someone who needs it. You might be surprised at the results!

### Speak it. Doodle it. Write it out.

Blessed are the peacemakers: for they shall be called the children of God.
—Matthew 5:9 KJV

### Say a prayer.

*Holy Spirit, help me to be a peacemaker. Where there are disagreements and division, give me your heart and wisdom to be a person who cares and listens. Amen.*

# DAY 59

# Comfort Matters

Some days are just difficult. You might feel sad or discouraged. Maybe you didn't make it on the team, or someone you love is sick. Perhaps you're in an argument with a friend, or you're missing someone who lives far away.

Life has hard times. This is why we learn to lean into God as our comforter. Matthew 5:4 says, "Blessed are those who mourn, for they will be comforted." It is blessed to mourn and to let tears flow. God comes to us in those moments and loves us where we are. He fills our needs with his love and grace because we are his children.

Have you ever gone to the beach and felt your stress and anxiety melt away? Or covered yourself with fluffy blankets when you were really cold? Watching the waves come to shore and crash onto the sand is calming, like God's comfort. Sinking your feet into the sand while those waves cross your ankles can remind you of his care. Tucking yourself under warm covers on a cold night brings to mind his relief and rest. These sensory parts of our lives remind us that God takes care of us and wants us to be loved and nurtured.

God provides and takes care of our needs. He is the one who knows our every weakness and gives us his comfort and peace. Try it today. Nurture yourself in a small way with a cup of tea or a bath. Allow his love to bring you rest.

### Speak it. Doodle it. Write it out.

Praise be to the God and Father of our Lord Jesus Christ, the Father of compassion and the God of all comfort.
—2 Corinthians 1:3

### Say a prayer.

*Holy Spirit, when life gets tough and I don't know what to do, remind me that your comfort soothes my soul. Help me give myself grace. Amen.*

DAY 60

# Chosen with Style

Styles and trends are fun, creative, and part of life. There will be fashion that comes and goes over the course of your lifetime, and you have a lot of choices for what to wear and why. Some people wear certain styles of clothing because it's comfortable, while others make decisions based on how they will appear to others. Your motivations for your style are important because, like it or not, people use clothing to determine what they initially think about you.

It's good to want to look presentable and to show your personality—as long as it doesn't overtake your identity or isn't inappropriate for the setting (you wouldn't wear a bathing suit to school, but it's entirely appropriate at the beach). What do you want to reflect about yourself by what you are wearing? Are you showing others that you care for yourself, are loved by God, and are creative? Or are your clothes reflecting other things like rebellion or a desperate need for attention? What is the motivation behind the trend you want to wear? God's love? Or the lust of the world? The fashion industry doesn't necessarily ask God for his opinions on the subject, but you can.

Take the opportunity to ask God about each piece of clothing as you put it on every day. Is it worth your wear? Remember that God cares far more about who you are and who you are becoming than what you wear. And the most beautiful you is the one chosen and loved by him.

### Speak it. Doodle it. Write it out.

Therefore, as God's chosen people, holy and dearly loved, clothe yourselves with compassion, kindness, humility, gentleness and patience.
—Colossians 3:12

### Say a prayer.

*Jesus, thank you for giving me the ability to choose to wear what I enjoy. Help me to make wise decisions about how to present myself to those around me. Amen.*

## DAY 61

# Diligence Is Good

Ever notice how good it feels to finish a lingering project? Focusing on tasks head-on with the tenacity and strength to push through the obstacles brings joy. When we use our skills and minds to do what God has asked us to do, we end up overcoming obstacles like procrastination, laziness, and fear. A diligent person is productive, and productivity can help us stay in tune with God. Being lazy can lead to grouchiness and mental turmoil. It can get us into trouble because laziness tends to be self-focused. But pursuing what is good and then following through on it brings great rewards.

Are there any chores or school assignments that you dread? Sometimes when we dread things, it helps to do them first or at least to get started on them. Work on the project for fifteen minutes. Maybe you'll hit your stride and finish right away, maybe you won't. Either way you'll have something done. Most often, when we finish what we need to do, we are fired up to accomplish the next important task.

So, the next time you find yourself not wanting to do a task that you know needs to be done, give yourself a quick pep talk and then get started! If you commit to fifteen minutes of work, you just might shift into motivation for the rest of the day. You'll be glad you did, and you will find that peace and productivity surround you.

### Speak it. Doodle it. Write it out.

So then, dear friends, since you are looking forward to this, make every effort to be found spotless, blameless and at peace with him.
—2 Peter 3:14

### Say a prayer.

*Father God, thank you for giving me a life to live! Help me to use my time in productive ways that serve you. Enable me to steward well the life you've given me. Amen.*

# DAY 62

# God Is Faithful

Lies about God are often easy to believe. We can forget that God is loving, kind, and faithful. It likely happens more than it should because we can quickly get caught up in our busy days, or by the latest social media buzz, or by the gossip that is making its way through the hallways at school.

We may see things we want and believe we should have them. If we don't have what we want, we can be quick to believe God isn't good. We give ourselves over to depression, sadness, and defeat when we forget God, when we believe lies that God is not as good as something else we want, or when we think that obeying him isn't worth it. Over and over again in the Bible, God reminds his people to believe in his faithfulness, and not to fall into the hands of the enemy by choosing things other than him.

When we search the Word and remember that Jesus is always faithful and always loving, that what he allows is for our good and for his glory, we can release our jaded opinions and the worldly concerns we cling to. We have a white-knuckle grip on so many things around us, sometimes without realizing it. Yet when we pause, purposefully inhale peace and exhale fear, we can be free from the entanglements of our minds and the worries of our hearts. When we trust God, we know that he will give us what we need.

### Speak it. Doodle it. Write it out.

For the Spirit God gave us does not make us timid,
but gives us power, love and self-discipline.
—2 Timothy 1:7

### Say a prayer.

*God, thank you for your faithfulness. Help me to let go
of the lies I believe and trust you. Amen.*

# DAY 63

# Grief Heals

No one likes when something sad or traumatic happens. In general, humans don't strive for conflict, but sometimes dangerous or dramatic things happen. People we love pass away, tragedy occurs, or accidents take place. Suffering is inevitable. So learning how to work through grief is not just important, it is essential.

When we are hurting or in trauma, if we make the time to slow down instead of speed up, we give ourselves the space to properly work through difficult feelings and needs. Slowing down means allowing those uncomfortable feelings to come to the surface, giving yourself space to be quiet or take a walk. It means intentionally allowing your mind and body time to rest and recover without quickly moving on to your next assignment or task. Perhaps you cook a warm meal, write down your thoughts, or find time to explore nature. These moments of slowing down can bring rest and beauty into your soul. It is good to take your time when thinking about where your heart may be hurting. It might seem easier to ignore the pain by covering it up with a quick fix, but grief must be attended to if recovery is to happen.

Slowing down also helps us remember that while we may feel alone when life seems to be falling apart, we aren't as alone as we think. Talking to a trusted adult can be such a gift when the world feels confusing or chaotic.

### Speak it. Doodle it. Write it out.

I have told you these things, so that in me you may have peace. In this world you will have trouble. But take heart! I have overcome the world.
—John 16:33

### Say a prayer.

*Holy Spirit, you are my comforter and counselor. Help me to remember to slow down when I am struggling and to be honest about how I'm feeling. Amen.*

## DAY 64

# Help My Unbelief

One day you might feel strong and confident. Life is smooth sailing, and everything seems to be in order. Perhaps your hard work paid off, you nailed a test, or you did really well at practice. During those times, your confidence grows. They are, in fact, good days, and they are a gift from God.

Other days, though, things might not go so well. Maybe you tried really hard at something and failed. Or perhaps you studied and studied, but you still don't understand your schoolwork. Days like this can cause unbelief to creep in, and it can be easy to doubt yourself or what God has called you to do.

Doubt happens to everyone, and even the disciples in the Bible struggled to believe with Jesus right beside them. When life gets tough, and you start to feel fear creep in, it's okay. It's not weak to struggle. To continue to move in faith, even when you are wrestling with fear, is strength. You are brave to do so! Remember that God is always with you and he loves you no matter what. You can simply agree with the prayer in Mark 9:24 that says, "I do believe; help me overcome my unbelief!" Say it out loud, several times if needed, and remind yourself of God's faithfulness to you.

**Speak it. Doodle it. Write it out.**

I do believe; help me overcome my unbelief!
—Mark 9:24

**Say a prayer.**

*Jesus, thank you for always being with me. Help me to believe in your faithfulness even when I doubt or feel afraid. Amen.*

# DAY 65

# Joy of the Lord

You'll have days when you've completely exhausted yourself. You might think you have nothing left to give, no more energy brewing, and you may even be so irritated that you want to throw in the towel. When these times come, and they will, it's important to remember that certain days God empties us of all that we have so that he can refill us with himself. It might feel like you want to quit, but don't give in so easily. Let him love you.

Our circumstances simply remind us that we are not the savior of the world, Jesus is. And we can rest and recharge in Jesus. After that breather, get back up! Celebrate how far you have come. Look at the finish line, and be determined to follow through. Think of all the times Christ has been by your side, cheering you on as you win and as you accomplish, as you do the work he's called you to do. These are important victories, and triumphant life in Jesus is meant to be honored and celebrated.

Take a few minutes today to make a list of several tasks that you have finished this week. They can be a big test or a simple chore. Maybe you even had a brave conversation with a friend, or you cooked something delicious in your kitchen. Hang that list on the wall in your room, reminding yourself to celebrate your accomplishments. Always remember that you can do it and to celebrate when you do.

**Speak it. Doodle it. Write it out.**

The joy of the Lord is your strength!
—Nehemiah 8:10 NLT

**Say a prayer.**

*Holy Spirit, thank you for your encouragement. Help me to recharge by resting in you and receiving from you. Thank you for your strength and the tenacity to finish. Amen.*

## DAY 66

# Serve the Little Ones

Ever learn a new skill and want to share what you learned with someone else? Or have you ever volunteered to help with kids or even worked as a babysitter? If you have, you know that you can find fun and encouragement in working with those younger than you. When you have gained experience or knowledge from a skill you have conquered along the way, it's great to share it with someone who looks up to you.

By helping children, you have the opportunity to encourage their hearts and minds and provide them with good and helpful tools that will serve them throughout their lives. Mentoring kids is so valuable! And serving someone else always helps lift our spirits too. Young kids need teens to look up to, just like you look up to adults or mentors in your life.

Jesus loves children, and he teaches us in Scripture that serving kids is one of the best ways to serve him. When little ones look up to you for care and support, you can be a person in their life who shows them the love of Jesus. Planting good seeds into their hearts is something to be proud of, and it's a worthwhile way to spend your time. Consider volunteering at church or with kids in your neighborhood. Pray for them, and watch them grow.

### Speak it. Doodle it. Write it out.

Then Jesus called for the children and said to the disciples, "Let the children come to me. Don't stop them! For the Kingdom of God belongs to those who are like these children."
—Luke 18:16 NLT

### Say a prayer.

*Jesus, thank you for the opportunities I have to serve children. Help me be a good example to all those I encounter, and show me how to be a positive influence. Amen.*

# DAY 67

# Kindness Wins

When someone is abrupt or says something unkind to you or about you, it can really ruin your day. You can end up mulling it over and over in your head, reliving the hurt or embarrassment until you're sick over it. Likewise, when someone says something kind or encouraging, it can lift you up and make your day light and happy.

What kind of words do you speak to others? Or even to yourself? Are your words soft and kind? Do you give grace and the benefit of the doubt? Or are you quick to judge and point the finger? Kindness is critical no matter the situation, whether we are speaking or responding. When we speak with grace, it can curb rudeness or rage instead of fuel it. In fact, your kindness will fuel kindness in others.

Find three people today who you can intentionally encourage with kindness. Cheer for someone, compliment a friend, or tell a teacher you appreciate him or her. Watch their responses when they are spoken to with grace. Did they smile or light up? Did they respond back to you with gratitude? What did you note, and why do you think it happened?

When life gets busy, when people are irritable, when accidents happen, or even when it's just a normal day, you can be kind and speak life.

### Speak it. Doodle it. Write it out.

Gracious words are a honeycomb, sweet to the soul and healing to the bones.
—Proverbs 16:24

### Say a prayer.

*Jesus, you are so kind. Thank you for speaking graciously to me when I need it most. Help me to guard my mouth and speak kindly to others. Amen.*

# DAY 68

# Be Real

When you look around, you will likely see a lot of advertisements, YouTube videos, and posts that include women who look like supermodels. Their hair is perfect, their makeup is freshly done, and their clothes are the most popular styles.

It's easy to see them and want to look like them. But real life doesn't look like the photoshopped and filtered photos online. The photo you see on the screen or in the ad is missing half the story. It's the half with a mess around it—the props, lights, and other belongings lurking in the background. Those things are all cut out in order to crop in a quick photo of someone who might look perfect at one angle. The photographer avoids all the other angles for one reason—the mess isn't attractive.

This phenomenon is not going anywhere, so it's really important to know that a filtered photo is not reality. You'll have days when you look and feel good, and those days are to be enjoyed. But you'll also have plenty of other days where your hair is frizzy, and you're wearing clothes with no name brand. God is with you in the frizz, the beauty, and everywhere in between. So relax and enjoy the God-given beauty of how he made you. Being a real person with real imperfections all day is real life, and it is good.

### Speak it. Doodle it. Write it out.

You are altogether beautiful, my darling; there is no flaw in you.
—Song of Songs 4:7

### Say a prayer.

*Father God, help me to guard my heart and eyes when it comes to social media. Remind me of your care and love for me, how you've designed me, and your peace. Amen.*

# DAY 69

# Be an Example

In everyday life, no matter where you go or what you do, people are always around you, observing how you live. While the idea can be intimidating, you are a walking example of God's values and your beliefs every single day. And this means that every day is important.

What you do is valuable. Your actions lead and teach others at all times. Never look down on yourself as having no purpose—because you do! By being present with those in your life—your siblings, parents, friends, or peers—you can shine a light in the dark. Looking friends in the eyes, putting away your phone, calling people by their first name, and listening without interrupting are a few ways to show others that you are present and available to be a good friend and a strong leader. Today, slow down and pay attention to how your family and friends respond when you are fully available to be with them.

When the Holy Spirit lives in you, you are a good example to anyone you encounter. His joy in you can change your environment when you walk in step with him. Sometimes it takes intentional tasks to live out our life with God, but in those tasks, we can grow and learn while also shedding light to those around us. Enjoy your day today, practice being present, and love those around you!

**Speak it. Doodle it. Write it out.**

The path of the righteous is like the morning sun,
shining ever brighter till the full light of day.
—Proverbs 4:18

**Say a prayer.**

*Jesus, thank you for a life that lives, loves, and is fully real. Let me be a light in the world, to share love and truth with everyone I encounter. Amen.*

# DAY 70

# Do What's Right

Ever been the only one to do the right thing? Choosing what is good over what is popular often feels isolating or even scary. Society and peer relationships can cause a lot of pressure to do what is less than godly, which puts you in situations where you'll sometimes have to choose what to do: make the right choice or possibly be rejected.

When you come across a situation where you need to stand strong, remember that Jesus was rejected for doing what God asked of him. Even though he was perfect, kind, and truthful, he was mocked because he stood up for those on the outside. Others were doing what they thought made them popular or powerful, but they weren't actually following God. The example Jesus gave was one of humility, love for his Father, and care for others. Do you tend to befriend those on the fringes? Have you ever needed to stick up for yourself or others because God asked you to? Think about those around you at school or in your extracurricular activities who are different from the status quo. Maybe he or she is struggling with an eating disorder, or lacks confidence in the classroom, or even wants to harm himself or herself.

Find ways you can show these friends support by encouraging them, helping them with homework, or going with them to get help from a trusted adult. You can be a person who supports others instead of belittling them.

### Speak it. Doodle it. Write it out.

But even if you suffer for doing what is right, God will reward you for it. So don't worry or be afraid of their threats.
—1 Peter 3:14 NLT

### Say a prayer.

*Heavenly Father, help me be the kind of person who loves well, even if I have to stand up to others. Thank you for caring for each person, no matter their need. Amen.*

## DAY 71

# A Season for Everything

Sometimes the answer is yes, and sometimes the answer is no. Have you ever gotten a no when you wanted a yes? One of the hardest things to do is acknowledge and feel your disappointment and frustration when you were hopeful for something to work out that doesn't. I don't know about you, but I tend to get angry, blame people for not coming through, or give up entirely and pretend like I didn't care in the first place.

God specifically addresses our struggle in Ecclesiastes, where we learn that everything has a season. Sometimes the answer is no because it simply isn't time yet, and other times the answer is no because God has something different and better planned. It takes trust in Jesus to be patient when we are disappointed, and having faith can feel uncomfortable. Trust stretches us to believe that God is in control, so we don't have to be.

The next time you feel the urge to be upset after a no or try to push something forward even though it isn't time, slow down. Observe your heart instead, delight and be grateful for small joys, embrace your mixed feelings, and then celebrate wins. I know it's hard, but truly making yourself wait for a better yes will be worth it. You can rest easy knowing that God has your yes covered. You'll see his abundant love for you when he brings that perfect gift at the perfect time.

**Speak it. Doodle it. Write it out.**

There is a time for everything, and a season for every activity under the heavens.
—Ecclesiastes 3:1

**Say a prayer.**

*Heavenly Father, help me in seasons of waiting and in seasons of going. Remind me that your timing is perfect, and you always have my best interests at heart. Amen.*

DAY 72

# Content in Jesus

Ever heard the saying "A Sunday well spent brings a week of content"? This quote explains that having a day of Sabbath rest will bring about the joy you need for the rest of your week. Too much work often makes us want more than we need. Intentionally taking some moments to refuel with Jesus will bring the rest we truly need.

Moving too quickly forces us into patterns that may not serve us well, and it does more harm than good. When we realize that true joy is found in walking with Jesus, step by step, whether that is swiftly or slowly, we find that we are always content. God gives us what we need for each part of the journey, and we can take life's ups and downs in stride. In doing so, we find the most satisfaction in Jesus himself, knowing that no matter what comes our way, we can be at peace with him.

Days of rest help us with this because they are a break from our normal weekdays. When you know that your day is to be set aside so that Jesus can work on your behalf, you learn a new lesson about his care for you. It's as if he brings you a free backpack full of supplies for your following week. Whether that's snacks, water, your favorite treat, or a blanket, he already knows what you need. You can become content in his provision when you practice abiding in Jesus.

### Speak it. Doodle it. Write it out.

But godliness with contentment is great gain.
—1 Timothy 6:6

### Say a prayer.

*Father God, thank you for satisfying my every need. Thank you for providing for me, loving me, and giving me strength in all circumstances. Amen.*

# DAY 73

# Silly Sometimes

There are times when life gets overfull or stressful, and you feel like you're going to lose it. I've been there. I think we all have. We have a lot of pressure and expectations, and those things can lead you to feel either really frustrated or really frenzied. It's almost like a case of cabin fever, but with additional overload.

One of the best things preschoolers do, and I did say preschoolers, is get their wiggles out. When was the last time you made a silly face? Or jumped around like a monkey? Told a funny joke or listened to a comedian? Laughing and joking around are good for the soul. And sometimes, we take ourselves too seriously because there is a lot of work to be done.

Don't forget to have a good time! Jesus took time to have dinner with friends, laugh with kids, and sing, and so should we. If things get a little too intense or stressful, you can jump up and down like a frog, dance in the rain, play a game of Twister, or get a book of jokes or Mad Libs. You are loved, and you can rest in the fact that God is in control. Take a minute to laugh, get silly, and breathe deeply today.

**Speak it. Doodle it. Write it out.**

Blessed are you who hunger now, for you will be satisfied.
Blessed are you who weep now, for you will laugh.
—Luke 6:21

**Say a prayer.**

*God, thank you for all the ways you provide for me. Help me to remember to relax, laugh, and enjoy your humor. You are good, and I can be reminded to be childlike in you. Amen.*

DAY 74

# Love Boundaries

Everywhere you turn, you'll find something that you want, or wish you had, or think you deserve. It's not wrong to want, but it is wrong when you go beyond your boundaries to get something you want. Boundaries are a gift from God to stay within the embrace of his love, protection, happiness, and provision.

When you go outside of those boundaries because you want to be liked or accepted, or because something or someone looks attractive to you, you can find yourself in a bit of trouble. Jesus didn't come to make rules for us. He came to earth to give us abundant life! The key to that abundant life, though, is staying within his guidelines, which are for our good.

Sometimes a quick fix might seem satisfying at the time, but the satisfaction won't last. And in the midst of it, you might get hurt.

Can you think of some boundaries you or your parents have set to keep you healthy? Perhaps you go to bed at a certain time each night, or you only have caffeine in the morning hours. In addition, what are some boundaries you may need? Though it takes self-control to say no, remind yourself that God's intentions for you are valuable. Set a few needed boundaries for yourself today, and celebrate a few wins that you've achieved because you had good boundaries in place.

### Speak it. Doodle it. Write it out.

Better a patient person than a warrior, one with self-control than one who takes a city.
—Proverbs 16:32

### Say a prayer.

*Father God, help me to be mindful of your boundaries. I want to practice self-control and patience while I live my life for you. Amen.*

# DAY 75

# The Shame Game

No matter how much you try to do the right thing, there will be times when you mess up. Maybe you say something rude you wish you hadn't, or you wear something you know your parents wouldn't approve of, or you spend time with a boy that you know you shouldn't. Guilt creeps up in red cheeks, a burn in your chest, or an irritating buzz in your body when you know you did wrong. So, what do you do? Do you hold it all in, hoping it goes away in time? That's probably not your best option.

What you can do is find your parents, a friend, or a mentor, and be honest. Let someone else into those feelings with you. Pray together, and confess your mistakes to Jesus, knowing that he is there to hear you, forgive you, and reconcile you. Then, let it go, and try to make new choices. Easier said than done, right? Because what often creeps up next is . . . shame.

Shame tries to keep you held down, even after you've experienced the grace of God. It might make you obsess over your mistake, or it might make you think that *you* are the mistake. Guilt convicts us so we can make changes, but shame plays the game of keeping us in jail. If you are experiencing shame, let your parents or friends in! They can shed light on the situation, and light expels the darkness. Remember that Jesus loves to forgive.

### Speak it. Doodle it. Write it out.

In you our ancestors put their trust; they trusted and you delivered them. To you they cried out and were saved; in you they trusted and were not put to shame.
—Psalm 22:4–5

### Say a prayer.

*Holy Spirit, thank you for both your comfort and your conviction when I do wrong. Keep shame away as I learn to release my mistakes to you. Please help me to be honest with those who love me and who can pray with me. Amen.*

## DAY 76

# Learning Differently

Every person on this planet is unique. God loves variety, and he created each of his kids to represent a part of his beauty, wonder, and intelligence. Some students excel in the classroom and others in school at home, some minds think in patterns or colors while others like concrete instructions. No matter where you fall in these categories, God made your mind good.

It can be easy to compare your learning style to someone else's with a completely different brain. As humans, we're always looking at our peers to understand what is happening in our world. It's true that some learning styles mesh better in certain learning environments, but problems can crop up when we start to think too highly, or not highly enough, of ourselves because we believe one learning style is better than another. That is truly not the case.

One way of learning isn't right or wrong, each way is simply different. What are some of the ways you learn? By taking notes or moving your body while repeating the math terms? Listening to the teacher or getting your hands in a lab? Write down your learning styles and celebrate them! Then find a friend with a different learning style. Talk about your similarities and your differences, and see what you can gain from one another. The next time you find yourself feeling dumb or superior while doing schoolwork, remember that everyone comes from a different life experience, and God made each individual equally special.

### Speak it. Doodle it. Write it out.

So God created mankind in his own image, in the image of God he created them.
—Genesis 1:27

### Say a prayer.

*God, thank you for making me unique! Help me to bless my mind with your Word and to value and appreciate the learning style you've given me. Amen.*

# DAY 77

# Detox

Every so often, people need a detox. Whether it's from sugar or media, certain foods or caffeine, or something else entirely. Too much of a good thing can be bad, and overabundance can take its toll. Ever notice how you can devour several donuts only to feel like you never want a donut again? Or have you ever had so much coffee that you got the jitters? And then your body just kind of crashed?

Or maybe your body is bothered by something that doesn't always bother others. If you've ever had an allergic reaction, you know that when your body finds something irritating, bumps break out on your skin or you get stomachaches.

Detoxing from overabundance or sources of irritation can radically change how you feel. Maybe a cleanse is in order for you! When we pinpoint and identify the things that trigger us, whether it's related to food or friendships, phones or chemicals, we can take the time to release those things from our daily lives. Maybe you'll be fine after a few days or weeks, or perhaps it's a long-term change. It depends on what it is and who you are.

Setting aside the time and discipline to detox is definitely worth the consideration. Can you think of something you might need to let go of? Either temporarily or even long term? Commit to clearing it out of your system, and see how you feel. Perhaps set a reward for yourself when you finish in order to encourage you to follow through. You can be sure that a reset will fill you with fresh energy and purpose, with more kindness and grace, and with a healthier version of you.

**Speak it. Doodle it. Write it out.**

Cleanse me with hyssop, and I will be clean; wash
me, and I will be whiter than snow.
—Psalm 51:7

**Say a prayer.**

*Holy Spirit, will you help me clear out what is not helpful in my life? Please
guide me into wisdom, boundaries, and fresh nourishment in you. Amen.*

# DAY 78

# Worthiness in Christ

There's a saying that goes: "Know your worth." But how exactly do you do that? Are we worthy if we perform well? Or if we are obedient? Are we worthy if we are pretty or popular? If you don't know what makes up your value, it's hard to know how to evaluate such a thing. If you don't have people in your life who are consistent in speaking truth and love to you, it can be easy to doubt who you really are in Christ.

Let me take a moment to say very clearly: You are valuable. You have great worth. And though we live in a society that sometimes values competition over comradery, taking constructive criticism as well as positive affirmation will help you be and grow into the wonderful person God made you to be. There will be seasons when you feel like an underdog or when you may struggle, but there will be other days when you light up the room with your grace and talent. On both kinds of days, you are worthy of love, kindness, truth, and grace. Your worth in Jesus never shifts or changes.

The next time you question your worth, ask yourself several questions. Who does Jesus say I am? Am I reflecting who Jesus says I am in my actions? What can I do to commit to integrity and growth in my current skills? Then, take a deep breath, and truly know your worth.

### Speak it. Doodle it. Write it out.

So do not throw away your confidence; it will be richly rewarded. You need to persevere so that when you have done the will of God, you will receive what he has promised.
—Hebrews 10:35–36

### Say a prayer.

*Jesus, help me remember my worth is in you. Remind me to be open and gracious when receiving feedback and affirmation. Help me to grow into a person whose life exemplifies your peace and purpose. Amen.*

# DAY 79

# Sadness Seasons

Sadness can drift into your life like a heavy cloak. Some days your energy may be low and life seems boring and purposeless. Unfortunately, depression is a big problem in our society as many people are hurting underneath a lot of difficult circumstances. Maybe that's you.

When unreleased feelings get stored in the body, it makes life seem unbearable and hopeless. That's when to get up and start moving. If you find yourself in a dark place and don't know what to do, hop up and get in the sun. Even if it's winter, head outside for a walk so those endorphins start flowing, call a friend, or clean your room. Eat something, get moving, and be with people who love you and need you.

When you battle sadness alone, you can feel hopeless or not important in a big world. But when you get with people and speak honestly, you'll see that your input, faith, movement, and creativity are needed in your community. No one is meant to do life alone, and taking steps to reach out, connect with your body through exercise, and find friends who are doing the same will fill you with purpose. You'll be ready to help serve the needs around you as you also serve yourself.

Before the next time you get stuck in a sadness rut, have your plan in place. You'll find yourself lighting up and lightening up at the same time.

### Speak it. Doodle it. Write it out.

You turned my wailing into dancing; you removed
my sackcloth and clothed me with joy.
—Psalm 30:11

### Say a prayer.

*Jesus, help me to remain in you. If I become sad or heavy with burdens,
remind me to call out to you and keep on moving. Amen.*

# DAY 80

# Integrity Satisfies

The world has always surrounded us with things that can pollute us. We're exposed to images or circumstances that steal from our hearts and minds or distract us from God. Some advertisements, movies, books, and songs try to lure people into something sinful. This defilement is both sad and disheartening. Keeping your eyes on Jesus when contamination is so easily available can be a difficult task.

But it's not impossible. You can choose to look away, find something better to do, or speak up for yourself when you're confronted with a situation that might steal your integrity. It might be an ad, or it could be the peer pressure of friends or a boyfriend. It might even be a TV series you feel uncomfortable watching even when everyone else seems to think it's okay or funny.

I can tell you this. There is nothing you see on TV or in others that will satisfy your curiosity, desires, or feelings of inadequacy the ways God will satisfy you. In the moment, I know it can feel the opposite. The pull to see what is going on in culture is strong. Yet God is always better, and the evil counterfeits can't get close to comparing to his love, peace, and comfort. So, breathe, think things through, look the other way, and say no. You've got this!

And if you made a wrong choice, the great news is our God is a God of forgiveness and restoration. If you think you made a wrong choice, ask for forgiveness, believe God has forgiven you, and continue pursuing what he has for you.

### Speak it. Doodle it. Write it out.

Don't let anyone look down on you because you are young, but set an example for the believers in speech, in conduct, in love, in faith and in purity.
—1 Timothy 4:12

### Say a prayer.

*Heavenly Father, in a world of defilement, help me to set my eyes on you and your creation. Give me eyes to see pleasure and your protection in the boundaries you have set. Amen.*

# DAY 81

# Garden Growing

Have you ever tended a garden or helped with one? I realize it might seem like gardening is for older women, ahem, myself included! I wasn't really interested in growing anything from the ground until I was in my late thirties, but once I started, I couldn't believe what I'd been missing.

Learning the patience and pruning of nature is a gift from God. God created the world and man in six days, and a beautiful garden was included. From the beginning, God valued land, growth, dirt, and the green we see all around us. Because of that, our lives in Christ can be nurtured when we spend time in gardens and with nature. When we watch a plant or flower grow, we enjoy witnessing God do something supernatural. The rain and sunlight produce something to eat, to enjoy, and to give our body nourishment.

If you've never tried nursing a plant or growing a flower, today is the day! Consider a trip to a local flower or plant shop, start small, and follow the simple instructions to care for your new potted friend. Watch your plant grow, keep a daily diary of your caretaking tasks, and jot down a few thoughts along the way. What happens when it is watered in the right increments? How does it look? On the flip side, what happens when you forget to water it? How is your relationship with God similar?

### Speak it. Doodle it. Write it out.

Now the Lord God had planted a garden in the east, in Eden; and there he put the man he had formed.
—Genesis 2:8

### Say a prayer.

*God, thank you for creating nature and the earth. Help me to tend to a piece of it, and teach me how to cultivate growth and patience through the process. Amen.*

# DAY 82

# I AM

Did you know that God has a lot of names? He surely does. Wonderful God, Prince of Peace, The God Who Heals, The God of Creation, and on and on. He is such a multifaceted Savior, and he's called the Beginning and the End. He's everything in between as well.

Throughout Scripture, God uses a variety of his names to convey to us a specific part of himself. If you have a sweater, you might describe that sweater as red or soft, maybe it's got flowing sleeves or a round collar. If you own more than one sweater, you might note that your other sweater is green with tighter sleeves and a V-neck. In the same way, God covers us with different characteristics like Wonderful Father or The God Who Heals. And when we receive or wear each part of his goodness through his different names, we get to experience more of the beauty of his provision of himself. He is thorough and amazing, and he meets every one of our needs with who he is.

Have you heard some other names for God? A few of them are: God Almighty, The Lord my Shepherd, The Lord is There, and Daddy. Do you have a favorite one? Why is that a favorite? Write it down in fun lettering, color it, doodle around it, and celebrate God's love for you.

### Speak it. Doodle it. Write it out.

God said to Moses, "I am who I am."
—Exodus 3:14

### Say a prayer.

*God, thank you for providing for me in many different ways. I want to know the names you give yourself because it will help me better understand your goodness. Amen.*

# DAY 83

# Hope Heals

Have you ever waited for something, and it felt like it was never going to actually happen? It's like when your family heads to the airport to go on vacation. You have all kinds of excitement moving through your body as you anticipate your time at the beach or in the big city. But after you get through the security checks and make your way to the terminal, you realize your flight is delayed . . . indefinitely. Ugh. So, what do you do in the meantime?

The Bible says that we can feel sick when we are in the place of anticipation. It can be hard to pass the time or not worry about what is going to happen. The unknown can consume our thoughts and fill us with anxiety.

But it doesn't have to be that way. During your times of waiting, prayer helps. When we talk to God about our concerns, he hears us and helps us let go. Walking while we talk to him is a great way to process our feelings while also getting rid of excess energy. It helps us become patient as we learn how to wait on his timing. Ask God for his grace and for patience and hope as you are delayed, and breathe through the tough moments. Even though most of us would rather choose a quicker route, God knows when we need to slow down and learn how to abide in him. He also knows when we need to go on vacation, and he makes a plan for that too.

**Speak it. Doodle it. Write it out.**

Hope deferred makes a heart sick, but a dream fulfilled is a tree of life.
—Proverbs 13:12 NLT

**Say a prayer.**

*Holy Spirit, you are so faithful to bring about patience in me. Remind me of your kindness and joy as you give me the peace to abide in you. Amen.*

# DAY 84

# Bite Your Tongue

People say rude things they don't mean. And sometimes they say rude things they do mean. Just like you will likely say regretful things you don't mean (and sometimes things you do mean). The tone in which you speak, as well as the tone in the way you respond, will have a significant impact on your relationships.

Life and death come from the tongue. That means you bring affirmation and kindness to someone with the same exact mouth that you bring hurt and disrespect. You can praise God with your voice and then immediately call someone a name. Hopefully that doesn't happen often in your life! We all make mistakes, but we can also all learn to pause before speaking to be sure what we say is kind. Who do you speak to most often? Your mom or dad? Brother or sister? When you talk, do they usually hear kindness in your voice or something else?

What you speak will determine whether someone receives value or hurt, grace or judgment. In a society where politics, religion, and all opinions under the sun can be cause for fearful attacks and rudeness, it's important to remember that what we say and how we say it matters.

How can you slow down today and be a voice for good?

### Speak it. Doodle it. Write it out.

The tongue has the power of life and death, and those who love it will eat its fruit.
—Proverbs 18:21

### Say a prayer.

*Jesus, place a guard over my mouth and peace in my heart. May I be slow to express myself when angry or annoyed, and may I speak life to those around me. Amen.*

# DAY 85

# Think of Others

There are few things more frustrating than being with people who only think of one thing: themselves. When you're hanging out with someone who only talks about the topics she enjoys or only wants to do activities that he likes, it feels suffocating.

The Bible teaches us to do the opposite: to think of others before thinking of ourselves. In Philippians, we are reminded to think the way Jesus thinks—not to get too puffed up with our own thoughts and opinions and to serve others before pushing to the front of the line. This can be hard in the moment. Especially when you're dealing with personalities that irritate you.

But when we serve Jesus, we can be patient and think of others before ourselves. We can outdo one another with honor by listening well, asking good questions, and showing others we care. We can practice remembering how God loves everyone, and that he died for every person with every personality type. Remembering this might also mean drawing a boundary to encourage space and rest. Thinking of others can mean both patience and limits. When we think of someone else and offer to be a good and faithful friend, we know that God is smiling down on us as well.

Put a few people in your life first today by asking good questions, responding to their need, or speaking kindly and candidly to someone who might bother you. Think through friendships that may need a truthful conversation or a boundary. Consider how you feel afterward, and thank God for giving you the opportunity to serve someone you otherwise may not have.

### Speak it. Doodle it. Write it out.

Do nothing out of selfish ambition or vain conceit. Rather, in humility value others above yourselves, not looking to your own interests but each of you to the interests of the others. In your relationships with one another, have the same mindset as Christ Jesus.
—Philippians 2:3–5

### Say a prayer.

*Jesus, help me to think of others before thinking of only my wants. Remind me that you care for me as I am caring for others. Amen.*

DAY 86

# Be Kind to Your Parents

Getting along with parents at this time of life can be frustrating. You're likely wanting more independence, wanting to be trusted with bigger things, and having a lot of feelings about it. You might think your parents are annoying and don't know much, but I promise they do.

If you have parents who are involved in your life and who are teaching you the ways of Jesus, you surely are blessed. Make sure to take the time to thank them and celebrate them. If you have parents who don't know Jesus yet or who might be struggling in their own lives, know that God is watching over all of you. He cares for you, and he cares for them. No matter what your family is going through, pray for your parents, and keep doing what you know God says is right. It will pay off, and God will be your dearest friend through it all.

No matter your circumstances, be kind and respectful to your parents. Honor their thoughts and healthy instructions. Encourage them, thank them often, and speak to them kindly. I know it feels easier to talk back if you're frustrated when they say no, disagree with you, or make you do chores you don't want to, but think before you speak. It will serve you well. How can you show your parents encouragement and love today? Honor them, as God has placed them in your life on purpose!

### Speak it. Doodle it. Write it out.

Be kind and compassionate to one another, forgiving each other, just as in Christ God forgave you.
—Ephesians 4:32

### Say a prayer.

*Father God, thank you for giving me parents and adults in my life. Help me to honor them with my actions and words. I want to be kind and loving. Amen.*

DAY 87

# Honor Your Body

You'll have many opportunities to take care of yourself throughout your life. You have choices on what to eat, what to drink, what to listen to or watch, whether or not to exercise, and whether or not to be physical in a relationship. Of course, any adult is going to tell you to make wise choices. Most are not trying to be killjoys but are hoping to spur you on to honor your body in all ways. Have you ever heard the verse in Scripture that our bodies are the temples of the Holy Spirit? This means that the Holy Spirit is always hanging out inside us. Does that blow your mind as much as it does mine?

Life in the Holy Spirit is one of freedom, comfort, conviction, and true health. Beyond the fact that the Holy Spirit is always available, we are the place where God should be worshiped. Taking care of ourselves spiritually, physically, and mentally honors God and honors ourselves.

Turn on some peaceful music, and slowly stretch your body. Allow your body and mind time to breathe and rest, to become healthy, whole, and vibrant.

### Speak it. Doodle it. Write it out.

Do you not know that your bodies are temples of the Holy Spirit, who is in you, whom you have received from God? You are not your own; you were bought at a price. Therefore honor God with your bodies.
—1 Corinthians 6:19–20

### Say a prayer.

*Holy Spirit, help me to honor my body in the way you have designed it. And enable me to be obedient to your guidance. Amen.*

# DAY 88

# Love Carefully

The word "love" is used pretty loosely these days, making it seem like being nice is love or tolerating everything is love, but that's not truly the case. The more you walk through life, you will start to realize that love in action involves surrendering, giving, and choosing. Love takes a lot of work. Even when you don't always want to, love is trying your best to give Jesus to others.

Though none of us are perfect, Jesus gives us opportunities to live like him every day. Love can be simple tasks in action like helping a sibling with homework, walking your dog, or doing the dishes for your mom. Love can also be deeper like forgiving someone who hurt you, or buying a gift for someone with your earned money. Loving someone else requires a level of giving because it means thinking of others more and ourselves less. Jesus loved us when he died on the cross to save us, though he had no sin of his own. What a gift!

Maybe you're trying to love someone right now who is difficult. You are not alone. This world is full of hurt and brokenness, and it takes time and practice to let the process of real love settle in our hearts and in the people around us. Pray for that person, be patient, encourage them, and let God transform and care for you and them while you do. Create boundaries and space if necessary, and seek additional help if needed.* I am proud of you for living like Jesus.

---

\* If you are in an abusive or dangerous situation, seek help from a professional, teacher, pastor, or the police.

### Speak it. Doodle it. Write it out.

If I could speak all the languages of earth and of angels, but didn't love others, I would only be a noisy gong or a clanging cymbal.
—1 Corinthians 13:1 NLT

### Say a prayer.

*Jesus, help me to love the way you do. Give me wisdom and joy in being a source of love to those I encounter, especially when it's difficult to do. Amen.*

# DAY 89

# Be You

There is only one you in the world! You are unique and beautiful, made in God's image to do what he has called you to do. Never forget that. The world will give you all the reasons why you don't stack up or why it feels silly to believe and follow Jesus. But none of those arguments are the truth. God has proven to be the best friend you can have, and he loves to see you shine in the world in your own way.

So when it gets tough out there and you're tempted to look for love and acceptance from the world around you, relax. What the world needs most is the Christ-filled joy of how God has worked in your story. Your hair, your voice, your face, and your body are the representation to the world of his goodness and creativity. We need you to be who he made you to be, to be truly you, so that his love and beauty can be on display through your thoughtfulness, your intelligence, and your heart.

Serve the body of Christ and the world with your life, gifts, and talents. Be humble, kind, gentle, and patient. Clothe yourself with compassion, work hard, and be fruitful. You are one of a kind, and this world needs you.

Write a list of ten things you love about how God made you. Choose your favorite verse from this devotional, and doodle it all over your journal page for the day. Celebrate! You are forever loved.

**Speak it. Doodle it. Write it out.**

For he chose us in him before the creation of the world to be holy and blameless in his sight. In love he predestined us for adoption to sonship through Jesus Christ, in accordance with his pleasure and will—to the praise of his glorious grace, which he has freely given us in the One he loves.
—Ephesians 1:4–6

**Say a prayer.**

*Father, thank you for creating me! Thank you for giving me life and breath, and thank you for giving me the opportunity to serve you every day. Help me live a life of gratitude and joy in you. Amen.*

# DAY 90

# Be Well

Life is eternal, and though your days on earth are numbered, they will mean more than you realize. How you live and walk with Christ will affect not only your life now but also the lives of those around you, and those who come after you.

You have amazing opportunities ahead, and in order to walk them out well, it's so important to be in step with Jesus. By taking the time out of your day to read this devotional, you are doing just that! Thank you for spending time here. The moments you spent growing and talking to Jesus over the last ninety days really matter. The small steps in life are necessary to train us, discipline us, and teach us how to move forward.

As you walk through the next few years, I hope you'll come back to this book to remember what God has done for you and to take the advice to heart again. The lessons inside, as well as your note-taking, will serve you well as you continue to learn to be loved by Jesus and love like him. Take a quick look back in your journal today. Relish all that he has accomplished in you during this time with him. Congrats for making it all the way through! Be blessed as you walk with him, allowing him the room in your heart to grow deeply and truly.

### Speak it. Doodle it. Write it out.

So then, just as you received Christ Jesus as Lord, continue to live your lives in him, rooted and built up in him, strengthened in the faith as you were taught, and overflowing with thankfulness.
—Colossians 2:6–7

### Say a prayer.

*God, you are the best! Thank you for filling me up and loving me well. Lead me as I grow, and continue to teach me how to live and love in you. Amen.*